Twayne's English Authors Series

Sylvia E. Bowman, *Editor*

INDIANA UNIVERSITY

George Borrow

(TEAS) 32

George Borrow

By ROBERT R. MEYERS

Friends University

Twayne Publishers, Inc. :: New York

Preface

Some writers have personalities so flamboyant that it is hard to separate the man from his work for purposes of objective literary judgment. George Borrow, nineteenth-century author of travel tales and romantic autobiography, was such a man. Like Lord Byron, whose place he was to take in the hearts of thousands of readers, Borrow was a solitary, magnificent wanderer. He amused himself on tour by playing linguistic tricks on astonished natives, drawing upon a store of extraordinarily wide, if superficial, language skills. He sought out gypsies and introduced himself as their brother, a mystic of the wind and the heath and a scorner of conventional men. Hiking twenty or thirty miles a day with ease, he hymned the praises of the open road and berated pedant philologists who breathed only the stale air of the study. With a potent right-arm punch and a strong staff, he gloried in encounters with vicious dogs and violent men. Six feet and four inches tall, with olive skin and flashing eyes, he cut a striking, memorable figure. He reveled in his prowess as a swimmer, once saving a man from raging surf and on another occasion diving into icy waters for a lengthy swim at the age of seventy.

It was inevitable that such a man should have provoked a society of admirers whose love for his bizarre personality would outrun discretion and blind them to many of his faults as a writer. Partly as a consequence of their strident affection, Borrow was so overrated for a few years that his decline was predictably sudden and severe. He dragged out the last twenty years of his life in such deep obscurity that even well-read Englishmen thought him long since dead.

Borrow's name is unknown to the general public and little known even in academic circles. The Borrovian Cult which once labored zealously to expand his reputation has deteriorated to a few isolated individuals who cherish their esoteric knowledge, and the Borrow books have only a slight sale in England and America. Teachers of the English novel course occasionally pay passing notice to Borrow, remembering him as the "gypsy man" who wrote *The Bible in Spain, Lavengro, The Romany Rye,* and *Wild Wales.* The first and last are described to students as travel accounts with a generous mixture of invention and exaggeration, the second and third as twin halves of a romantic autobiography with more factual data than seems likely at first reading. All four contain passages as lively as any writing done in the period; they also descend, frequently, to stiff and pedestrian prose which only a dedicated Borrovian can wade through with patience. In either case, the student who reads them can experience the joy of surprise; no eager high school teacher has here anticipated his university colleague.

If the student seeks information on Borrow from the standard reference sources, he finds little. Albert C. Baugh's *The Literary History of England* devotes one-third of a page to Borrow in a total of 1,605 pages of text. Ernest A. Baker's massive *History of the English Novel* has only three brief footnotes on Borrow, and Baker explains the lack of other reference in several thousand pages of text on the basis that Borrow is not a novelist at all but a travel writer and autobiographer. The question has been much argued, but perhaps Baker is not entirely correct. Lionel Stevenson, for example, places *Lavengro* and *The Romany Rye* within the tradition of the English novel, particularly the picaresque (*The English Novel* [1960]). He finds, as others have, a unifying structure in the two books; and he says that "under the apparently casual surface there is an integration of recurrent themes and interlocking situations."

But apart from the academic arguments, it is clear that the extraordinary esteem in which Borrow was held during the middle of the nineteenth century has faded. The Borrovian Cult perished quietly between the two world wars. Even the Borrow House Museum in Norwich was disbanded after World War II. All that remains are copies of a publication of that name, written in 1927 as a guide for tourists and admirers, by G. A. Stephen. The city librarian in Norwich, a village closely tied to Borrow's life, writes that little use is made of the material in his stacks. During the past decade few serious inquiries have been received each year. The considerable collection of Borrow manuscripts there are infrequently requested and then "chiefly from motives of curiosity rather than research." Brian Vesey-Fitzgerald's biography is still read occasionally in the Norwich library (It was issued three times in 1962, for example.), but the librarian says with the caution of an experienced bookman: "Even this use may well have been inspired by school examinations."

Borrow's books are not displayed in drugstores or on the shelves of popular bookstores. A Collins Classics edition of *Wild Wales* appeared in 1955, Everyman's Library reissued the same book in 1958, and MacDonald Illustrated Classics issued *The Bible in Spain* in 1959; but they sell poorly. John Murray, Borrow's publisher, writes from London that, although Borrow is well remembered around the place, his books have slight sale. Only two are still on the Murray publishing list, *The Gypsies* and *Romano Lavo-Lil*, of which they sell between ten and twenty copies a year. According to book catalogues in England, about twelve publishers have Borrow books on their lists, mostly cheap editions, indicating the continuance of some slight market.

Occasional articles appearing in magazines betray no strong current of enthusiasm. Hiking and camping devotees in England and America no longer invoke Borrow's name to justify their communions with nature. The Gypsy Lore Society still regards Borrow as an important gypsy authority, according to the American secretary; and frequent articles about him have appeared in past issues of their publication. But the secretary admits that some regard him as a romanticist full of "the wind on the heath." His mystic approach to gypsy life has little appeal for those who favor the straight-facts, no-nonsense approach of modern sociological studies.

But the memory of the eccentric gypsy-lover lingers. A student does a paper; a scholar writes a dissertation. John Kieran, in his *Treasury of Great Nature Writing,* honors Borrow by printing his famed *Lavengro* passage on the viper. Sir John Hunt interrupts his July, 1954, *National Geographic* account of the conquest of Mount Everest to tell of spending one whole afternoon, high on a dangerous slope, relaxing with Borrow's *Wild Wales.* Allan Gilbert prefaces his popular *Literary Criticism* text with an extract from *Lavengro* in which Borrow scoffs at pedantic philologists and commends the active life as the proper preparation for enjoyment of an epic.

There are many other references to Borrow by writers whom students and general readers are likely to encounter, including a matchless parody of his style by Arthur Conan Doyle. But the fact remains that Borrow is not in the first rank of English writers, and one who intends to make his acquaintance needs some such rationale as has been provided by Lionel Trilling:

One might spend one's life pleasantly and profitably with the secondary writers of the English nineteenth century, the writers whom no one would think to call "great," the odd, quirky spirits from George Borrow to Mark Rutherford, the travellers, the autobiographers, the essayists, the men who had a particular, perhaps eccentric, thing to say, and said it fully and well, with delight in what they were doing and no worry about greatness. (*The Griffin,* June, 1955, p. 6)

If the reader is willing to get off the main-traveled roads and to company with the odd and quirky George Borrow, he will find memorable moments. In that conviction, this book is written.

A condensed biography of Borrow is combined in the opening chapter with an introductory account of his major works. Because Borrow's books are not well known, a summary is given of the more important ones. Critical reaction to these works is represented in a survey of British, French, and American periodicals which devoted space to Borrow during his creative years, roughly from 1840 to 1862. Copious extracts are brought together to provide a comprehensive statement of the meteoric rise and fall of Borrow's popularity. The witness of contemporaries other than critics and the figures for book sales in England and America are cited to illustrate Borrow's erratic journey across the literary horizon.

There are three principal elements in Borrow's books which made him appealing to his Evangelical, nonconformist audience: the travel motif, the extensive moralizing, and the pervading impression of a flamboyant and unique personality. These are analyzed, and illustrations are taken generously from Borrow's books. The travel narratives made him instantly popular because they were presented as fact rather than fiction, because they were picaresque in spirit and structure, and because they were intensely nationalistic. For the Bible Society, whose agent he was in Spain, and for the Evangelical audience he obviously had in mind, no more appealing trio of attributes could be imagined.

Borrow's moralizing and religious pronouncements leave much to be desired from the modern point of view, but they delighted large numbers of his mid-Victorian readers. His use of the stereotyped language of piety, his prudishness, and his lack of concern about consistency or about the profound religious issues of his time are shown to be part of his brief, but immense, popularity.

The examination of his striking personality is no less significant in understanding that popularity. His romanticism about gypsies, his almost unbelievable self-confidence, his virulent anti-Catholicism—these constituted his charm until the public mood changed. Even the contradictions in his personality lent an aura of romance until they were finally seen to be partially willful and perverse.

Much evidence exists to show that Borrow had the craftsman's concern for his compositions. He made pronouncements upon other writers (generally not happy ones); he accepted counsel from those he admired; and he revised material with some diligence. His prose style changes with different subject matter—sometimes felicitously, sometimes ruinously. As a story-teller, he is often superb; seldom is he a complete bore. His powers of description are considerable; his characterizations are memorable when he chooses to make them so. The colloquial style of his narrative sections, the heavily ornate style of his moralizing moods, the Celtic dreaminess and sentimental melancholy of his ultra-romantic spells—these are illustrated and examined to provide materials for assessing Borrow as stylist.

It was by no means accidental that Borrow should have become a distributor of Bibles in Spain. He grew up with the diction and melodies of the Authorized Version of the Bible in his ears. His use of these idioms and rhythms contrasts strangely with the roguish jargon and robust narration which mark the major part of his best work. Since Borrow passes into and out of the Biblical style abruptly, an attempt is made to determine whether there is any rationale which prompts him to drape the Biblical idiom over some areas of subject matter.

An examination of Borrow's relationship to other writers concludes the study. Amazingly isolated from the literary giants of his own time, Borrow has nothing to say of Arnold, Carlyle, Ruskin, Thackeray, Browning, or Tennyson. He castigates Scott's "Popery" and Wordsworth's dullness but impercipiently in both cases. He gloried in his highly eccentric reading, which left him ignorant of his contemporaries but knowledgeable about the most obscure of Scandinavian poets. He was, nevertheless, strongly influenced by Defoe and mildly influenced by Fielding, Smollett, Sterne, Dickens, and Bunyan. Traces of Borrow's influence upon succeeding writers are found in the work of George Meredith, Theodore Watts-Dunton, Robert Louis Stevenson, Maurice Hewlett, and others.

The task undertaken is analytical rather than defensive. No good purpose is served by pretending that Borrow belongs in the canon of classics. But he deserves something better than the current neglect of his books, and closer acquaintance with him will lead most readers to agree again with Mr. Trilling that Borrow is one of the "first-rate secondary figures in our literature." As such, he seems to merit examination.

ROBERT R. MEYERS

Wichita, Kansas
January, 1966

Contents

Chronology

1803   George Borrow born July 5, at East Dereham, Norfolk.

1803- Constant movement as father's regiment maneuvers over
1812   Midland counties. Formal studies sporadic, but many eccentric persons and exciting events crowd Borrow's rich boyhood.

1813   Regiment sent on 250-mile march to Edinburgh, where George receives some of his best schooling in the famed High School attended and praised by Walter Scott.

1815   Regiment in Ireland after Napoleon's escape from Elba. George studies at Clonmel, where he meets the Irish boy Murtagh who teaches him Erse for a pack of cards. A lifelong love of horses and languages begins.

1816- Family at Norwich, the village which came nearest to being home for George during his childhood wanderings.
1824   Schooling continues until 1819, when George is articled to a Norwich law firm. He meets William Taylor, philosopher, agnostic, and iconoclast friend of Southey's, and learns German from him. Begins making translations of Scandinavian poetry, publishing some in *The Monthly Magazine* in 1823. Taylor writes Southey that his teen-age friend already understands twelve languages.

1824   The elder Borrow dies, and George leaves for London in early spring to work for Sir Richard Phillips, a publisher. He writes critical notices of new books, translates from German, and compiles six volumes of spicy reading from the *Newgate Lives and Trials,* a case-history of notorious crimes and criminals.

1825   Unhappy with Phillips and hackwork, Borrow makes walking tours of the island. The famed fight with the Flaming Tinman probably occurred during this summer, as well as the Isopel Berners episodes.

1825- Returns to Norwich a commercial failure to begin the so-
1833   called "Veiled Period." Continues work on Scandinavian translations; wanders in Britain and probably in Europe. Does hackwork for booksellers and newspapers in Norwich in 1827. Translates Scandinavian poetry again in London in 1829.

1833   Takes Bible Society job and is sent to St. Petersburg to make Bible translations.

1833- In Russia, with headquarters at St. Petersburg; works on
1835   the assigned task but follows any exciting linguistic by-path which turns up.

1835- Returns to England, from which the Bible Society promptly
1840   sends him to Portugal for similar work. Moves into Spain in 1836 and does some five years of Scripture-circulating there.

1840   Returns to Oulton, with his new bride, Mary Clarke.

1841   Publishes *The Zincali,* a hotch-potch collection of gypsy stories, songs, and word definitions.

1843   Publishes *The Bible in Spain,* an account of the Spanish adventures and Borrow's most popular book in his own lifetime.

1851   Publishes *Lavengro,* a romantic autobiography of Borrow's early years.

1853   The Borrows move to Yarmouth, from which point they begin numerous walking tours. A tour of Wales in 1854 was the genesis of a later book, *Wild Wales.*

1857   *The Romany Rye* completes Borrow's autobiography.

1860   Family moves to London, where Borrow plays literary lion to a diminishing audience and mines the linguistic lode for occasional articles.

1862   *Wild Wales,* a return to the successful travel-narrative genre which had made Borrow famous in 1843.

1869   Mrs. Borrow dies at seventy-three; Borrow is sixty-six and virtually forgotten by the public.

Chronology

1874   *Romano Lavo-Lil,* a gypsy wordbook. Borrow returns to the old family home at Oulton.

1874-   The declining years, marked by ineffectual attempts to re-
1881   new old friendships. Most of his countrymen had believed him long since dead when Borrow died quietly in 1881.

CHAPTER 1

The Road and the Study

EVERY writer is shaped by his childhood, but few to so obvious an extent as was George Borrow. His father, who boxed with enthusiasm and unusual skill, joined the Coldstream Guards after flattening a village constable; Borrow's earliest memories were of wanderings with the regiment over the British Isles and of stories of strong men handy with their fists. The exigencies of military life during the Napoleonic years caused the guards to move often, and Captain Thomas Borrow transported his family from barracks to barracks during his son's adolescence. Proud of having fought and of almost having defeated Big Ben Bryan, later British boxing champion, Captain Borrow convinced his son that it was advantageous to use his fists dexterously, to read the Bible often, and to dabble with philosophy. Wanderlust, delight in physical prowess, the melodic rhythms of the King James Version, and the pleasures of superficial philosophy—these were the stuff of Borrow's youth; and they are never long absent from the books he wrote in maturity.

Born on July 5, 1803, in East Dereham, Norfolk, Borrow's schooling was desultory except for a period in Edinburgh when he studied at the High School. Wide travels and colorful soldier talk influenced him far more than the classroom and gave him the ingredients which set him apart from other writers. He met gypsies early and was fascinated by their wild, free ways and strange tongue. In Ireland he fell in love with horses and riding, a lifelong romance which later provoked some of his finest prose. His travels stimulated an interest in languages, and he developed an uncanny ability to fall in with people willing to teach him. Many have observed that Borrow was a linguist rather than a scientific philologist, but it is possible to go too far in disparaging his skill with languages. Though not a specialist, he did have extraordinarily

[17]

wide acquaintance with tongues which the masses have always marveled at and would marvel at today.

In his twentieth year, Borrow went to London to try the literary life. His misadventures there in 1824 with publisher Sir Richard Phillips are vividly told in *Lavengro*. Borrow disliked his publisher (he came close to having a penchant for hating anyone above him in authority), and he caricatured him savagely in the book. There is no question but that Borrow's spleen was overactive. Phillips, according to accounts of him, seems to have been a rather mild-mannered fellow given to metaphysical speculation. Borrow's direct, overbearing manner probably rubbed him raw. Worse, Borrow had nothing suitable to peddle on the literary market; and Phillips was a businessman. He insisted that Borrow stop beating the drums for Danish ballads and do sensible things like book reviews and the turning of criminal records into readable prose for sensation seekers.

A few months of hackwork and some fits of deep melancholy (the "horrors" of which Borrow speaks occasionally) put an end to the London dream, and Borrow escaped in a predictable manner. He set out in 1825 on walking tours of England, indulging in the favorite activity of his life. Undoubtedly, many prototypes for characters who appear later in his books crossed his path during these months.

He returned home to Norwich a failure, with no occupation and none in view on the near horizon. The succeeding years, from 1825 to 1832, have never been well documented. Borrow omitted the period from his autobiographical novels, perhaps because it was a time of considerable anguish. His friend Richard Ford urged him to tell the public about the "Veiled Period," but he refused. It may be that he enjoyed throwing the romance of mystery over years of grubbing. He traveled during these years, although probably less than he liked to hint later; and he spent much time in Norwich and London doing hackwork for pocket money.

Borrow could never get over the idea that the public was hungry for Gaelic bards and Scandinavian ballad-singers, and in 1829 he was in London working on his translations. The British Museum in 1831 turned down his proposal to enrich their archives by his translations, but he still believed that sooner or later the northern muse would excite the public. He persisted in this error until he died.

He worked feverishly in 1831 to get employment abroad, under the auspices of the British government, or any government, touting his language skills as his chief endowment. This led eventually to a job with the Bible Society, which decided to send him to the Russian capital of St. Petersburg to manage the circulation of a translation. His famous twenty-seven and one-half hour walk to London from Norwich took place at this time. Borrow boasted that a roll of bread, two apples, half a pint of milk, and a pint of ale fueled him for this feat.

He studied the Manchu language in London for half a year and went to Russia in the early summer of 1833. He spent two years there, diverting himself with the problems of his assignment and thrilling over odd dialects and difficult translation jobs. The Bible Society rewarded him upon his return by shipping him off to Portugal in the fall of 1835. For several years thereafter, Spain was the center of his activity and gave him the material for his most successful book.

During a period of residence in Madrid, Borrow renewed an old friendship with Mary Clarke, widow of a naval officer he had once known; and it was not long before busy tongues were recounting a romance. Some had Mrs. Clarke chasing Borrow, others had Borrow chasing her considerable fortune. Whatever blend of friendship, physical charm, and financial need may have motivated him, Borrow paid court to his old friend; she responded; and they decided to return to England and marry. There was a brief delay when Borrow, with his affinity for getting into touchy situations, irritated a passport official and landed briefly in jail. Infuriated as always by lack of proper respect for his person, he involved everyone he could in Spain and in England in his fight to punish the offending official. He left Spain in April, 1840, having spent a total of five years in and about that country. His bride-to-be was on the ship; they were married April 23, in Cornhill. The Bible Society, long harassed by this unpredictable man, complimented him for his work and said it had no further use for him. He and his wife settled down on her estate at Oulton. Borrow was thirty-seven, a year younger than his father had been when he married.

Life at Oulton was quiet. Borrow could walk the marshlands and hear the surf of the North Sea, and he enjoyed the attentions of a wife who was companion, nurse, and secretary. There was time now for the writing of longer works, and Borrow turned author in earnest, publishing in 1841 his first book, *The Zincali; or, An Account of the Gypsies of Spain, with an Original Collection of their Songs and Poetry, and a Copious Dictionary of their Language.*

I The Zincali

The Zincali, a formless account of Spanish gypsies, was printed in two handsome volumes by John Murray of London, but 750 copies proved to be enough. Despite the strange mixture of poetic and prose passages, of dictionary notes and casual anecdotes, several reviewers spoke well of the book. But not quite three hundred copies had been sold in June, two months after publication; and a year later Murray was deploring the poor sales in England, while admitting that the "Yankees" had printed two editions, one of them selling for twenty pence. Murray, who blamed the political situation for poor sales at first, argued that no books were selling well at the time; but later he accepted the fact that the book was not likely to appeal to a wide circle of readers.[1]

Composed from the notebooks Borrow had kept during his wanderings in Spain, *The Zincali* is an introduction to gypsies generally and to Spanish ones in particular. Borrow ranges widely, discussing habits of Russian, Hungarian, and English gypsies, and he gives an account of their migrations. He has not yet found his best manner, and the book is little more than a catalogue; but touches of the later Borrow style vivify many of the chapters. One of his stories in the opening chapter begins with this comment, typical of Borrow's later interest in prizefighting and in the out-of-doors: "When a boy of fourteen, I was present at a prize fight; why should I hide the truth? It took place on a green meadow, beside a running stream. . . ." Had there been more such beginnings, the account of the gypsies of Spain would have sold better.

The main body of the work details minutely the lore Borrow had acquired about Spanish gypsies. He writes of their beliefs about the capacity of some to cast the evil eye upon others, about their dress, about the tricks and practices of their women, and about their moral character. He attempts a brief collection of their poetry and a study of their language, and he concludes with a glossary of gypsy words.

The *Athenaeum* expected a warm reception by the public and praised Borrow's originality by saying that a "new subject is perhaps, at this age of the world, a godsend, beyond the hopes of publishers or critics." [2] *Blackwood's Edinburgh Magazine* gave thirty-seven pages of extracts from the book, commending Borrow's "entertaining pages" and concluding that the work was "certainly more novel and interesting than three-fourths of the books of travels which crowd our libraries." [3] *The British and Foreign Review* permitted Richard Ford to devote nearly fifty pages to *The Zincali*. Ford, who might have been tempted to use Borrow's book as a foil for his own traveler's guide to Spain, was generous. He praised Borrow's originality and hoped for more from the "agreeable historian." [4] Similar remarks in other English, German, and French periodicals gave Borrow a boost; he became generally known as a student of gypsy life and as a linguist.

The haphazard anthology would, however, send shudders down any modern philologist's back; for Borrow had inadequate knowledge of the language and depended on a helper who provided, for the most part, gypsy slang. Even the title word was soon challenged for accuracy of inflectional form. Fortunately, the book has enough of Borrow's idiosyncrasies, odd enthusiasms, and quaint digressions to merit one look by a man with leisure time. The best thing about the venture, for Borrow, was that he got some belated advice from Richard Ford, whose handbook on Spain had long been standard. Ford appreciated Borrow's eccentricities, and he saw that the reading public would like a book which mirrored them. He urged Borrow to write another book, giving much more of his time to dramatic situations in which the author was the central figure.[5] The advice was too late to help *The Zincali* overcome some of its defects, but there is no question but that it helped Borrow succeed enormously with his next book.

II The Bible in Spain

The Bible in Spain, the second major effort, appeared in December, 1842, although it is dated 1843. The premature appearance was probably a concession to Borrow, who was chafing to see the book in print. The Bible Society had agreed to let Borrow use the letters he had written home to it during his Spanish visits, and a large part of the book is composed of material in those documents. There are, however, some reminiscences which Borrow would never have sent back to his serious-minded employers.[6]

The book made Borrow famous overnight. Its blend of religious zeal and thrilling adventure made it a welcome guest on bedside stands in the homes of Evangelicals. There is no question but that the great success of the book was due principally to the fact that its hero was on a religious pilgrimage, a missionary enterprise. Many of its readers could not have accepted in good conscience a mere fiction or a purely secular travel account; but a fascinating story of godly enterprise was a different matter. The landscape of Spain rises from Borrow's pages with impressive vividness; a veritable parade of rogues and rascals, priests and politicians, brigands and revolutionaries march across it. It must have been wondrous for the Evangelical reader to justify unaccustomed, pleasant sensations by remembering that the hero was God's agent. Brusqueness and dubious machinations that were to seem unforgivable of Borrow in later books were excused in this one because he was on God's work.

The travel account opens with the hero already at sea and bound for Lisbon. Within a few sentences, a sailor speaks of a premonition of his death, and within a few more lines, he is lost in a raging storm. "Truly wonderful," concludes Borrow, "are the ways of Providence!" It was the right note to strike for his readers, who were often as puzzled as he to account for life's queer accidents, and he remembers his missionary character often enough to keep readers from being embarrassed by a bald recitation of events unconnected with the ways of God.

Plot is all but non-existent, although Borrow occasionally encounters characters met earlier in the book. Borrow, the tall Englishman with the Bibles in his knapsack, is properly appalled at the ignorance of scripture on the part of natives, at the callousness of their priests, and at the clumsy bungling of some who have preceded him to spread the Word of God among a benighted

people. Yet he never loses for a moment his keen relish for the
infinite variety of the Spanish landscape, nor his contagious delight in the splendid ingenuity by which he outwits any who try to
frustrate his mission. Often in peril and near defeat, he always
triumphs. Usually he remembers to give credit to God, but not so
often as to detract from the picture of himself as an all-conquer-
ing, self-reliant hero of God.

The narrative fairly gallops along, with little of the sermonizing
that occasionally clogs the later books, although he may pause at
any moment to exclaim over scenery or to moralize about the
brevity of man's life. Borrow likes the people of Spain, despite
their religion; and he loves their rugged, brooding land. Although
he describes with delight the cutthroats who put him often in
peril, he refuses to believe that the Spanish are vile as a nation.
But vignettes like the following are ultimately the memorable features of his book: the drunken muledriver who killed his beast,
then mumbled inanely that it was God's will; the Manchegan
prophetess who made Mr. Brandram, Secretary of the Bible Society, so angry; the pig-merchant who whipped out his wicked-
looking knife in the inn at Badajoz; the Spanish hero Quesada,
who stopped a revolution in Madrid for one whole day and had
his severed fingers used to stir coffee in a cafe that evening; the
mutely religious goatherd who affirmed his faith in God by staring
at the sun; the "children of Egypt" who tried to tempt Borrow into
a horse deal at Duenas; and the treasure-digger, Benedict Mol,
who reappeared at times to give a thin thread of plot to the book's
structure. The account ends with rather disconcerting abruptness,
but it has had God's plenty of exciting adventure long before.

It is no wonder that Borrow encroached sensationally that year
upon the long-standing, stable popularity of Walter Scott and
Charles Dickens. Dickens, actually, was Borrow's most serious rival because he was still exploiting a new taste in fiction. But even
Dickens had fallen victim to one of those sometimes inexplicable
sloughs of public apathy just about the time of publication of *The
Bible in Spain. Martin Chuzzlewit* was published during 1843-44
in twenty monthly parts, but it fell far short of all expectations of
sales.[7] Dickens was still far from unpopular, but his hold had
slipped enough to irritate him considerably and to call for some

strenuous exertions on the part of Chapman and Hall, his publishers. It was into this momentary vacuum that George Borrow slipped with his perfectly timed tale of travels in Spain.

The book was a best seller, running through several editions in an expensive three-volume form. The official British guide to best sellers for the century is Desmond Flower's *A Century of Best Sellers*, published by the National Book Council in 1934. It does not list the best seller for 1843, but Samuel Lover's *Handy Andy* is named for 1842 and Disraeli's *Coningsby* for 1844. The omission is frustrating, but the assumption which some Borrow students have made that his book was the best seller for that year seems safe. Murray sold 3,796 copies of the three-volume edition in 1843; two printings of the Home and Colonial Library series sold 7,584. The total number sold in 1843 from these three printings was 11,380. Thirty thousand copies were sold within six months of publication in America, but Borrow got none of the profits.[8]

Princes, bishops, ambassadors, and members of Parliament began to praise Borrow, and his fame spread to neighboring countries. In 1844 a German edition was published, a French edition following in 1845. There was an abridged version in Russian. Despite minor variations in accounts of the sales, one fact is clear: Borrow was triumphant in 1843.

And the critics agreed completely with the public. Reviews were filled with praises for Borrow's style and content. An *Athenaeum* comment is typical: "We are taking our leave of a genuine book . . . we earnestly hope that we have not rambled our last in Mr. Borrow's company."[9] But *Tait's Edinburgh Magazine* touched more surely upon a public nerve when its reviewer spoke of Borrow as the Christian adventurer:

There may be different opinions as to Mr. Borrow's merits and qualifications as a Missionary of the Bible Society; there can be none as to his having produced a clever, most amusing, and to minds capable of healthy intellectual assimilation, profitable work. We trust that it will not be the last, and that his gipsy lore, and the singular freemasonry which might find him safe way into many inviting regions, sealed to ordinary Christians, are not to be henceforth lost to the world.[10]

Some reviews stressed Borrow's striking appearance and physical bravery; others admitted that the colporteur did not always seem to have the humility an agent of the Bible Society should have. Readers were repeatedly promised that they would meet in Borrow's pages no sedate, disciplined religionist but an extraordinary traveler who found exciting adventure at each turn of the road. Only the *Dublin Review,* an ardently pro-Catholic publication, attacked Borrow; but, his strong anti-Catholic bias stirred by the review, he reacted typically in a letter to his publisher Murray in August of 1843: "It is easier to call names and misquote passages in a dirty little *Review* than to write *The Bible in Spain.*"

High praise came from France, where one reviewer thought Borrow threatened to dethrone Smollett and Dickens, and another found the book worthy of the best picaresque novelists of the time. Borrow was giddy at the thought of such fame. His letters to Murray and others at this period are exultant and childlike. He could not bear to hear that sales had dragged, even for a month; he was, he told his wife, "the star of the morning." [11]

American reviews echoed the praise of British and Continental reviews. Even the *U. S. Catholic Magazine,* although attacking Borrow's bigotry and cant and warning that the name in the title was not indicative of the *spirit* to be found in the book, praised Borrow's tale as one filled with "romantic adventure and glorious description." [12]

The title of the book aroused considerable comment, both then and later. One reviewer felt that, although the book was "blameless and admirable," it perhaps went too far in making the name of the sacred book a part of its title. [13] Jane Findlater, years later, called it "perhaps the most ill-advised title that a well-written book ever laboured under, giving as it does the idea that the book is a prolonged tract." [14] But Augustine Birrell probably shared Borrow's view when he said that a boy reader, curled up on a Sunday with a book approved by his unsuspecting parents because of its title, doubtless "blessed the madcap Borrow for having called his romance by the sober-sounding propitiatory title of *The Bible in Spain!*" [15] Borrow surely was aware of the tastes of his Evangelical and non-conformist readers; only such a title would ever have gotten some of them into his exciting pages. They must have been surprised, these grave, pious readers of Bible Society publications, when they found that many of Borrow's adventures had little to do with the Bible. But once the initial shock was past, many could doubtless have said with William Dean Howells that "the religious interest is lost in the excitement of the personal adventure." [16] Borrow's title was a lucky one.

The book continued to be popular through the late nineteenth and early twentieth century. Samuel Smiles advised readers of his *Brief Biographies* in 1860 to read the book at once, if they had not.[17] Augustus Jessop, in 1893, described a devoted following Borrow had among Cambridge students.[18] And Jane Findlater described *The Bible in Spain* in 1904 as "to this day far the most popular of Borrow's books." [19]

Borrow's name was so well known after his recital of the Spanish tours that Sir Robert Peel, speaking to the British Parliament in April, 1843, paid him the great compliment of assuming that the mere mention of his name would be an easily understood synonym for perseverance and courage.[20] Flushed with success, Borrow promised Murray that he would begin work on a book which would surpass *The Bible in Spain* in excellence and popularity. He hoped to finish it within a year, but it went slowly while he played the literary lion and wrestled with his recalcitrant muse. An encounter with a snobbish aristocrat was enough to put him in a rage for weeks. He was sometimes boorish at dinner parties, and his growing restlessness and irritability alienated many who had admired him. He spent nine years writing his third book amidst quarrels with his neighbors about pet dogs, gloomy beliefs that the public was forgetting him, and rage when the quiet of his estate was disturbed by the laying of a railroad through it.

The scheme this time was simple. He had decided to satisfy those reviewers who had exclaimed over his colorful personality and had urged him to disclose more of it. His book was an autobiography; but, since there were exaggerations in it, he soothed his stubbornly Victorian conscience by referring to it as a "dream." There were some vacillations about the title (the book was first called *Life: A Drama*), but *Lavengro—The Scholar—The Gypsy —The Priest* was decided upon and the book appeared in February, 1851.

III Lavengro

Casting himself as Lavengro (word-master), Borrow begins at the beginning with his place and date of birth and with a sketch of his parents. He cannot claim noble blood, but he assures the reader that men with less ability than his soldier father had become generals and that his mother was a blend of gentle beauty, ardent Protestantism, and undying love of the Bible. He admits that he was slow to read and speak, but he quickly relates how portents of his future greatness were recognized by others. One of these portents involves Lavengro's meeting with the king of the vipers; it is unforgettable.

Lavengro's boyhood is enriched by discoveries of old Danish skulls in a village church, by colorful marches to fife and drum by his father's regiment, and by the rapture of opening for the first time the pages of an illustrated copy of *Robinson Crusoe*. His first meeting with gypsies is a triumph; they are about to chuck him into the nearest pond when he displays the tamed snake he carries about in his shirt. Soon after, he meets the gypsy boy, Jasper Petulengro, who calls him "brother" and vows they will meet again.

In Ireland, after one of the many moves of his father's regiment, the hero meets Murtagh, a sixteen-year-old native whose fingers cannot forget the deck of playing cards he had once shuffled so joyously. Lavengro sees his chance and offers to trade his own deck of cards for tutoring in Irish. Within a few weeks he is speaking the language, and the amateur philologist is embarked upon a lifelong pursuit.

He rides his first horse in Ireland, a magnificent animal that scatters foam and pebbles to left and right as he trots along at the rate of sixteen miles an hour. Lavengro is hopelessly lost in another passion: "People may talk of first love—it is a very agreeable event, I dare say—but give me the flush, and triumph, and glorious sweat of a first ride, like mine, on the mighty cob!"

Lavengro attempts to learn law, but it is a futile enterprise for one who longs so ardently for gypsies, fighting, horses, prizefighting matches, and wind on the heath. He has a humorous encounter with the pedant poet named Parkinson, who says that Lavengro suffers from a lack of Classical education and has no talent for poetry. Lavengro refuses to believe it, and the law books turn ever dustier and duller to his eye. The lure of languages is too strong to resist, even before the pipe-smoking philosopher, William Taylor, helps banish the last vestiges of interest in legal affairs. Taylor, who thinks the Germans are a philosophical race *because* they smoke, is one of Borrow's finest character sketches.

The hero wonders at eighteen whether all is not vanity and vexation of spirit. He asks himself whether his translations of Welsh and Danish poetry may establish his reputation for a thousand years, gives this up as too optimistic, then consoles himself by the thought of what he may become by age forty. He toys with the notion that all is illusion, that he has not even been born at all. But he quickly rejects what he calls "Berkeley's doctrine-Spinosa's doctrine," saying that these are ancient lies from all men who would be as wise as God.

Recovering from such moods, he listens to a colorful Methodist preacher on the heath and later by the roaring sea. Sober of mien and plainly dressed, the preacher is electric with the passion of proselyting; and Lavengro is momentarily aroused to dedicate his life to such service. But the mood passes and an incomparable talk follows with Jasper Petulengro, met once again as he often is in the book. The gypsy talks poetically of the wind on the heath, and he tries to make his brother mystic feel what a sweet thing it is to be alive.

On the death of Lavengro's father, the hero goes to London to seek his fortune. He is promptly greeted by a rakish bluff who says, "One-and-ninepence, sir, or your things will be taken away from you!" Borrow stares the insolent fellow down, then muses on the philosophical import of what has just happened. He decides that there may be other such greetings in the big world, but he knows the counter-sign: he clenches his big fist harder than before.

He visits Sir Richard, the publisher, in the hope of interesting him in translations of ancient Scandinavian ballads. The publisher disdains such material, but he invites the stranger to London to do various kinds of hackwork. Lavengro meets in Sir Richard's office a droll, dry clerk named Taggart, whose most obvious dedication is to his snuff box. One of their conversations shows Borrow at his best in the vein of wry humor:

"Well, young gentleman," said Taggart to me one morning, when we chanced to be alone a few days after the affair of the cancelling, "how do you like authorship?"

"I scarcely call authorship the drudgery I am engaged in," said I.

"What do you call authorship?" said Taggart.

"I scarcely know," said I; "that is, I can scarcely express what I think it."

"Shall I help you out?" said Taggart, turning round his chair, and looking at me.

"If you like," said I.

"To write something grand," said Taggart, taking snuff; "to be stared at—lifted on people's shoulders—"

"Well," said I, "that is something like it."

Taggart took snuff. "Well," said he, "why don't you write something grand?"

"I have," said I.

"What?" said Taggart.

"Why," said I, "there are those ballads."

Taggart took snuff.

"And those wonderful versions from Ab Gwilym."

Taggart took snuff again.

"You seem to be very fond of snuff," said I, looking at him angrily.

Taggart tapped his box.

"Have you taken it long?"

"Three-and-twenty years."

"What snuff do you take?"

"Universal mixture."

"And you find it of use?"

Taggart tapped his box.

"In what respect?" said I.

"In many—there is nothing like it to get a man through; but for snuff I should scarcely be where I am now."

"Have you been long here?"

"Three-and-twenty years."

"Dear me," said I; "and snuff brought you through? Give me a pinch—pah, I don't like it," and I sneezed.

"Take another pinch," said Taggart.

"No," said I, "I don't like snuff."

"Then you will never do for authorship—at least for this kind."

"So I begin to think—what shall I do?"

Taggart took snuff.

"You were talking of a great work—what shall it be?"

Taggart took snuff.

"Do you think I could write one?"

Taggart uplifted his two forefingers as if to tap; he did not, however.

"It would require time," said I, with half a sigh.

Taggart tapped his box.

"A great deal of time; I really think that my ballads—"

Taggart took snuff.

"If published would do me credit. I'll make an effort, and offer them to some other publisher."

Taggart took a double quantity of snuff.

Forced to put aside his dreams about the great work and the ballads, Lavengro compiles instead the *Newgate Lives,* a labor which whetted the real Borrow's interest in criminal types and vastly increased his ability to write racy, pungent prose. He is exposed to practical experience when a petty gambler asks him to be a bonnet, or cover man, for the old thimble-and-pea game. Lavengro rejects the offer and discomfits his tempter by declining four Armenian nouns.

Lavengro periodically succumbs to the "horrors," a deep melancholia which had gravely frightened his parents in his adolescence. He has a seizure just before meeting Isopel Berners, also called Belle, whose unrewarded adoration of Lavengro has won her universal sympathy among Borrow readers. Lavengro fights an epic battle with the Flaming Tinman, winning finally when he uses the "Long Melford" (his right-arm punch) which Isopel has stridently insisted upon from the sidelines. Winning Belle in the bargain, Lavengro tarries with her in Mumper's Dingle and the two of them study Armenian. A statuesque Scandinavian type, Isopel seems fashioned to be the mate for the tall, athletic Borrow; but he commits the unpardonable sin of absolute purity and bores her half to death. She weeps readily when her hero tells of his dangerous adventures, and she submits tearfully to his punishments when she fails to pronounce the Armenian numerals properly. Borrow assures his Victorian readers that he lived with her as a brother; he hurries Lavengro back to Armenian verbs whenever that hero becomes uncomfortably aware of Belle's splendid qualities as a woman.

Lavengro and Belle talk several times with the Man in Black, a renegade Catholic priest who discusses religion endlessly with

Lavengro and scoffs at the gentility of the English aristocracy. The cynical priest is made to say such things as: "What have we to do with what the founder of the Christian religion cared for? how could our temples be built or priests supported without money?" Obviously a straw man for Borrow's anti-Catholic prejudices, the priest stumbles off drunkenly, mumbling vicious slanders against true religion.

Lavengro continues to tantalize poor Belle. He teaches her to decline "master" in Armenian; she tells him that he tempts her to make him decline "mistress" in English. Lavengro says, with that half-savage humor often typical of him, "I decline a mistress." A postillion shares their dingle briefly and tells them one of the longest tales in the book. The end of his story and his decision to sleep in the dingle with them that night bring to a close one of the strangest volumes in Victorian literature.

Once again, the vignettes scattered through the autobiography are memorable. One treasures the memory of Lavengro's visit to Stonehenge and his talk with the shepherd guide there; of the Welsh preacher, Peter Williams, who suffers agony over his conviction that he had committed the unpardonable sin in boyhood; of the quiet Quaker met on the banks of a fishing stream near Norwich; of Lavengro's first view of Marshland Shales, the great English trotting horse, to whom the hero tips a hat that he would not doff to earl or baron; of the Byron funeral cortege (a "glittering lordling," true, but author of "Childe Harold and that ode," and so not to be forgotten among men); and of many other sketches.

Despite abundant proof of literary skill, *Lavengro* failed with the general public and with the critics. Apparently, the public had passed through the Byronic phase and had buried itself in other matters. Borrow's wandering hero could not compete with David Copperfield, with laureate Tennyson, or with Thomas Carlyle, fulminating thunderously in his "Latter-Day Pamphlets." Borrow's love of the open road, of horse-witches, and of apple-women was too far removed by this time from the sudden spurt of social idealism, the controversies over political liberties, the Manchesterism or Kingsleyism of the time.

Losing the brief happiness he had known from the success of the Spanish adventure story, Borrow sank into lasting bitterness.

He raged against the two or three reviews which he had read and which damned him for romanticism and lyricism. His subsequent bitterness was so great that it gave rise to legends among his friends that *Lavengro* had received no favorable reviews at all. The truth is that only one-third of the notices were really hostile, but admittedly, these were vitriolic enough to burn a much less tender ego than Borrow's. Adverse critics held that the book ranged from almost puerile sentimentalism in some places to extraordinarily violent abuse in others of the people and the institutions Borrow hated. They took offense at Borrow's calling the book a "dream" instead of an autobiography, feeling that he was mysterious only to protect himself from criticism; they pled for less of the marvelous and fantastic and for more of the masculine adventures which they had celebrated in *The Bible in Spain.*

The *Eclectic Magazine* found the book "exceedingly unpleasing" and decried the "ale-house brawls" and "vocabulary of the tents." [21] The *English Review* felt that the one appropriate comment for the whole of the book would be, "How very odd!" and found it more filled with trash than with amusing matter.[22] The *Athenaeum* saw the book as a collection of sketches which counted for nothing since the narrative was incoherent and poorly articulated.[23]

So went the hostile reviews. They were not completely fair, but Borrow's boastfulness and eccentricities had irritated critics; and they now condemned some of the very techniques they had praised nearly a decade earlier. When the book sold poorly, Borrow blamed the critics. Three thousand copies were printed first, but twenty-one years were to pass before another edition would be required. As for Borrow, he never recovered from the scars left by rankling words and poor sales. He had already found society dull and sometimes irritating in England after the Spanish tour, but the poor critical reception of *Lavengro* provoked him to vicious hatreds. It was an abnormally embittered man who sat down to vent his spleen in the supplementary volume to his autobiography or "dream."

During the writing, Borrow had to leave Oulton in 1853 because of his wife's health. They went to Yarmouth to live in rented rooms for seven years, using them as a base for excursions over the island. Borrow became increasingly obsessed with his hatred for gentility. His biographers relate instances of his ingenuity in insulting people whom he considered affected. He was also increasingly given to the "horrors," those deep fits of melancholy which he appears at times to have indulged and enjoyed with the romantic excess of his nature. It was in such a context that he penned his attacks against aristocrats, Catholics, fickle readers and critics, and personal enemies.

John Murray, who worried about the splenetic qualities of *The Romany Rye*, refused to publish it as Borrow sent it in. Borrow threatened to turn it over to another publisher, but he finally revised some passages at Murray's insistence. The publisher reluctantly brought the book out in May, 1857.

IV The Romany Rye

The second half of Borrow's autobiographical novel is much more deliberate than the first. The entire book covers only a few weeks; Borrow dwells leisurely upon the characters who people his pages. Lavengro has become Romany Rye ("gypsy gentleman"). It is convenient in discussing this book to use Borrow's own name, although a character in the story refers to him on one occasion as "Mr. Rye."

The Romany Rye opens with daybreak in the dingle and with the postillion fast asleep, worn out, no doubt, from his lengthy story which had closed *Lavengro*. Borrow nods politely to Belle when he awakens, then begins forging a linch-pin on his anvil. He playfully strikes a spark at Belle, and she leaves when it alights upon her knee. The postillion eats Belle's breakfast with warm praises for her skill, accepts the linch-pin from Borrow, and appears to be all set to kiss Belle goodbye when she draws herself up menacingly and chills his ardor. It is as near to a kiss as Belle ever comes in either half of the autobiography.

The Man in Black returns to the dingle to discuss religious history at length. Borrow plays innocent and asks for a description of the Pope and of the intricacies of Catholicism. Belle refuses to serve the priest more drink when she decides he has had enough, but she admits that she cannot evict him from Mumper's Dingle, a free gathering place for wanderers of all kinds. The priest suggests that Belle might become a nun; with her customary pungency, she threatens to break her glass against his mouth if he continues in that vein. The discourse winds on lengthily with the Man in Black representing Catholicism in a way Borrow knew would delight his Evangelical readers and would infuriate ardent Catholics.

Then the parade of characters begins. A gypsy woman named Mrs. Chikno upbraids Borrow for living in the dingle with Belle "without being certificated"; she calls this conduct "the roving line" and only with difficulty accepts the hero's demurrer. Borrow, after this talk, may have been stirred; he goes home after breakfast and gives Belle another lesson in Armenian.

The gypsy family, the Petulengros, comes to visit and to talk of its travels. Borrow's "brother" Jasper arrives later, and the dialogue between the two men is splendid. Borrow never writes better dialogue than he does for these scenes. A high point in the early part of *The Romany Rye* is Borrow's talk with the gypsy girl Ursula, whose insistence upon the singular virtue of females of her race provokes Borrow into philosophical musings as to the reason.

After thirteen chapters, the Armenian studies pall for Belle; she declares that she is weary of such nonsense and prefers a kind word. The hero offers to go off to America with her to conjugate the verb for love, the "prettiest verb" in the Armenian language, *siriel*. He would leave priests, humbug, learning, and languages behind, he says; and he magnanimously offers to wrestle Belle, recalling that Brynhilda would not marry the man who could not fling her down.

The next morning Belle is cold and reserved. As the hero leaves, he promises that, unless she has made up her mind about his proposal, there will be another lesson in Armenian, however late the hour. As he looks back, Belle stands in the early morning sunlight and slowly returns his wave. Borrow says abruptly, "I never saw Isopel Berners again." Soon afterwards he receives a letter from her in which she explains, in rather stilted language, that she feels he is mad and that, although madmen are said to make good husbands, she prefers not to think that she has taken advantage of his infirmity. She tells him to fear God, to take his own part, and to tip folks the "Long Melford" when it is necessary. Borrow seems forced when he laments his wounded pride and debates about following Belle to America. He appears to put her out of his narrative with almost an air of relief. So ends one of the most bizarre episodes in all of English literature.

From this point in the story, Borrow becomes a wanderer and talker who meets a procession of interesting characters. The vignettes, as usual, make up for lack of causal connections and careful plotting. Borrow meets a man who has fallen asleep in a meadow while reading Wordsworth's poetry; Borrow recommends it as a soporific. The postillion turns up again, as does the Man in Black; Borrow seems to weave them into and out of his story only for purposes of a surface unity. He manages to be flung off a horse and knocked senseless, a happy accident which results in his being cared for by an old man who is full of long, strange tales and who is as ardent about learning Chinese as his crippled guest is about other languages. Borrow even encounters a jockey who had once been bested in a fight by Belle Berners herself, a coincidence which carries little conviction for the reader. Even Murtagh, who in *Lavengro* had taught Borrow Irish for a pack of cards, turns up unexpectedly. The meetings appear contrived.

Nothing in *The Romany Rye* is livelier than its Appendix. Borrow had been goaded to fury by the critics of *Lavengro,* and he creates an opportunity to pay them back. Disdaining to prick, slice, or sting, he bludgeons his various foes with a massive club. He begins by justifying Lavengro, despite that character's fondness for ale and the company of gypsies. The old Borrow scorn for nobility of lineage is rampant; the true gentleman may be just such an unknown and eccentric wanderer as Lavengro was.

Then the tempo speeds up. He assails Rome again, scoffs at the fondness of English pseudo-intellectuals for foreign nonsense, and rips into Scott for assisting in the resurrection of Popery from its near burial in England. He cudgels teetotallers and those who have no taste for fistfights, and then he passes on to his low point in the section entitled "Pseudo-Critics." The final chapters of the Appendix are so violent and hysterical that admirers of Borrow wish he had not written them. He concludes by praising *Lavengro* for all the wrong reasons and by seeking belatedly to convince Englishmen that it was composed "for the express purpose of inculcating virtue, love of country, learning, manly pursuits, and genuine religion—for example, that of the Church of England." He apparently did not know where his book's real merit lay, or else the rejection of it had stung him so deeply that he was beyond caring. There are few addenda in the history of English literature so peculiar as the Appendix to *The Romany Rye;* if it were gone, we should be deprived of some of the most extraordinary vituperative writing in our language.

But for Borrow's immediate public, the book fell dead from the press. It had been six years since readers put down *Lavengro,* wondering what was going to happen in the dingle on the morning after the storm which closes that book. The wait had been too long; the public had lost interest. Critics who bothered to notice *The Romany Rye* at all were extremely hostile to it. The *Saturday Review* denounced Borrow's "coarse satire," his "great defects," and his savage Appendix; the reviewer advised the writer to return to the freshness and liveliness of style which had made the Spanish adventures so charming.[24] The *Athenaeum* recalled the "clear, fresh and decided" prose of *The Bible in Spain,* with its "descriptive power," "poetic vividness of colour, and a substratum of fact and probability which encouraged acceptance," and it mourned the loss of all of these in the new work. "No author," it said, "to use a gipsy phrase, has *drabbed* so much *drao* into literary dough as the author whose preparation we have now read." [25]

The Appendix sealed Borrow's fate. It cut him off from all but the most ardent friends, and it turned critics against him for life. Its attempt to defend *Lavengro* against critical rebukes, its wild unreason about priestcraft, its jingoistic nationalism, its scoffing at gentility nonsense, and its blaming Walter Scott for the Romanist revival were too much for sober readers. Believing that Borrow was now simply a man crazed with hatred, they scoffed at the book with the critics and decided simply to forget the gypsy man.

Borrow left Yarmouth in June, 1860, to move to London, where he lived in such seclusion that he was unknown to more than a handful of old friends. He translated a few poems from Russian, Danish, Turkish, and other languages; but the public was indifferent. In 1854 he had made some walking tours in Wales with his wife and stepdaughter. As the fever of hatreds subsided within him and as he saw how foolish he had been, an old love for Wales revived and was tempered into a mellowly delightful book, *Wild Wales.*

V   Wild Wales

Appearing in 1862, *Wild Wales* was what the critics had hoped might follow *The Bible in Spain*. Borrow, a wanderer again, cocked his ear for strange words and captured vividly the colors, sights, and sounds of the Welsh countryside. All who think that Borrow was truly Celtic in spirit find in that faith an explanation for his triumphal tour of Wales and the charming book which resulted from it. The land becomes one of enchantment as Borrow sketches it. He does not try to analyze or dissect; he is content to respond not only to the beauty of mountains, lakes, and streams but to the charm of the people.

Borrow begins *Wild Wales* by candidly revealing to the reader how he tricked his wife and daughter into going to Wales rather than to some fashionable resort ("there was nothing I so much hated as fashionable life," he told them). The trio set out upon their adventures, and the book returns to the style of *The Bible in Spain*, except that the daring Bible distributor has been replaced by a mellowed gentleman, accompanied by his family on a tour of strange but friendly country.

A typical chapter finds the three Borrows hearing a fine sermon on "Tares and Wheat," one which they agree over lunch is one of the best they ever heard. Later they visit a Methodist camp meeting, with "plenty of vociferation, but not one single burst of eloquence." One of the Methodist preachers pleads for teetotalism, at which Borrow laughs. He leaves the meeting to visit a rude peasant family who plead with him to give them God, whether he be priest or minister. They admit to doing wicked things besides their tinkering, and the wife reminds her husband how he is "sometimes haunted by devils at night in those dreary Welsh hills" where they are going. Borrow offers them money, but they shout they have plenty of that. "Give us God! Give us God!" they howl after him as he walks away.

Borrow is in no hurry in this book; the pace is even more leisurely than it had been in *The Romany Rye*. The old animosities seem to be gone, but the ability to create lively character sketches remains. Borrow can now speak calmly of Scott and praise his lyric "Norman Horseshoe" as one of the most stirring he knows. It is perhaps fitting that Borrow should close with a final analysis of some linguistic phenomena of the Welsh language. He poses questions about relationships between Welsh and Sanskrit, counsels that human reason cannot answer, and says that men should turn humbly "to a certain old volume, once considered a book of divine revelation, but now a collection of old wives' tales, the Bible."

The hero of *The Bible in Spain,* too eager for a fight and a thrill, has come finally to this quiet, conventional admonition to his countrymen. But by now, no one cared. The book was simply ignored by readers and by most critical reviewers. Those who did comment were apparently eager to pounce upon any defect and were quite willing to overlook the merits they had praised so lavishly in the Spanish account. A scathing rebuke from *Cornhill Magazine* reflects the attitudes of the few critics who noticed *Wild Wales* at all:

The book is extremely defective, and contains an unpardonable proportion of triviality and self-glorification. Really it is too much to demand that we should read the record of every glass of ale which Mr. Borrow drank—usually with his criticism on its quality—or be patient under the fatiguing triviality of, "I paid my bill and departed," which occurs incessantly; the more so because, while he is careful to inform us that he paid the bill, he never once mentions the amount; the detail he records is superfluous, the details he omits would at least have been serviceable to future travellers. Snatches of commonplace conversation, and intensely prosaic translations of Welsh poems, swell out of this book, and render it rather tiresome reading.[26]

Wild Wales is a better travelogue than cavils of this kind would suggest, but irritation with Borrow had hardened into a permanent posture for the literary critics of England.

Borrow was now sixty, with twenty more years to live; but he was cut off completely from a public which had idolized him for a short time. He walked, buried himself in books, and made notes for articles. In January, 1869, his wife died; and he was left alone, his stepdaughter having moved out of the household when she married in 1865. Borrow found out then what others had known before: that he was almost utterly dependent upon his wife. He found solace in the old philological interests and renewed his old fascination with gypsies. His last book, *The Romano Lavo-Lil,* or *Word-Book of the Gypsies*—as unreliable as *The Zincali* had been in its philology, and with much less vigor and quaintness in it—appeared in 1874. Only the confirmed Borrovian would search through it for one of those vignettes which Borrow could still occasionally compose with skill.

Few men in the history of English literature have risen with such triumphant suddenness to success and then fallen, well before death, into such obscurity. It took dedicated friends to bring the Borrow name back to life and to touch off a brief revival of interest in the early twentieth century. One of them, Theodore Watts-Dunton, Borrow had captivated in 1872. Watts-Dunton remembered years later how he had related some anecdotes about Borrow to a Sunday afternoon literary gathering in the early 1870's. The stories were well received until he mentioned that he had but recently talked to Borrow and walked with him, at which point his hostess let him know that his "character for veracity had suffered," since the man in question had been dead for many years.[27]

Borrow, returning to Oulton, tried to renew a friendship with Edward Fitz-Gerald, with whom he had spent pleasant hours in earlier years; but Fitz-Gerald thought it was foolish at their age to put up with each other's company, or indeed anyone's company, and resisted. Borrow puttered about his deteriorating estate, sat in a favorite chair in the Norfolk Hotel, made pronouncements to those who would listen, and slowly faded. He bitterly resented references to his age, for his mind had outlived his great physical strength. His death came while he, at seventy-eight, was alone in his house on July 26, 1881. The public was not moved.

CHAPTER 2

A Bourgeois Byron

BORROW'S great popularity in 1843 and for several years after
was the result of three elements in his books which appealed
powerfully to his Victorian readers. His loss of popularity was
due to changes in techniques and to his festering hatreds and
open calumnies. Since *The Bible in Spain* everywhere exhibits all
three elements and with the least diminution of their effect, it is
not surprising that it should have been Borrow's one greatly successful book.

The elements, not necessarily in order of importance, are the
constant emphasis upon travel and adventure, the presence everywhere of a strongly moral and religious tone, and the omnipresent
appeal of a flamboyant personality. It was inevitable that all of
these should have been touched upon in the survey of Borrow's
reception by the critics and by the public. But they can profitably
be isolated and examined in greater detail, a step which will, in
turn, carry this study into a consideration of the ways in which
these elements modify Borrow's prose style.

Two of the principal motifs of Borrow's books are directly in
the Byronic tradition and the other is, from the viewpoint of the
Evangelical middle classes, an impressive reversal of another element of Byronism. Byron, whose fame was again momentarily
fanned high by his death in 1824, was the hero of the upper
classes. Not that the middle classes or those below them did not
recognize the magic of his name or the romance of his life. But
they could not, because of their Evangelical piety, concede these
things openly. Byron was a heroic figure to gaze upon with wonder, not one whom they could take without reservation to their
hearts. But in Borrow they found legitimatized some characteris-
tics which had made Byron internationally famous. Byron had

traveled into remote and dangerous places; so had Borrow. Byron's colorful personality, filled with paradoxes, had drawn men to his writings and had found expression in varied stylistic techniques; the same was true of Borrow. The reversal mentioned earlier lay in the difference between their approaches to morality. Where Byron had lived licentiously, at least from the non-conformist viewpoint, and had employed some specious philosophizing (in *Cain,* for example) to justify it, Borrow presented himself to his public as a virtual ascetic in matters of sex. His philosophizing was conventional to the point of triteness, but it reiterated the doctrines of Evangelical belief and was generally prim and puritanical enough to win complete approval.

The Victorian masses of the 1840's suddenly had upon their hands a bourgeois and respectable Byron, a hero whom they could take to their hearts with no feelings of guilt. Borrow satisfied their appetite for adventure and at the same time he made it clear to them that his daring forays were sanctified by a high and holy mission. Nonconformists could read about cutthroats, gypsies, and thieves without feeling that they were idling precious time away because the man who was recounting his perilous life among these scoundrels had, after all, gone there to distribute Bibles and to preach Protestant Christianity. And the great admiration of the masses for a personality of heroic dimensions was now made religiously acceptable because the hero, acting for God, remembered occasionally to bow humbly and to profess his subjection to the Creator.

So, for the average churchly reader in the early 1840's, Borrow was a new manifestation of the national hero—an exciting personality uncursed by Byronic guilt complexes, but blessed instead with an amazing assurance of his moral and religious correctness; a far-traveler fleeing not, like Byron, in disgrace from his country, but taking her Holy Scriptures with her blessing to a benighted land; a finder of adventure, not in the seraglio or private bedroom, but in the lonely and dangerous mission fields to which God had called him.

There is no evidence that Evangelicals actually linked what they liked in Borrow with what had been fascinating in Byron; but as one ponders the three elements which made Borrow's books famous, it can be seen, without pressing the comparison, that Borrow really did stand in the limelight as a new Byron—with a difference.

I *Travel*

From Anglo-Saxon times to the present, travel literature has always been popular among English readers. But the flood tide was probably reached during the nineteenth century. The Romantic emphasis of the late eighteenth and early nineteenth centuries had stressed one of man's moods: the desire to escape from the familiar in favor of the remote and exotic. The demand for accounts of journeys to Africa, Asia, and the Western world was so great that practically anyone who had made such a visit might see his tale in print.[1] Prose and poetry were both used; Byron's *Childe Harold* was enormously popular in 1812 when Borrow was nine years old. Borrow, growing up in the midst of this avid taste for travel literature, knew he could hardly fail to please with an account of his trips.[2]

In the midst of a flood of travel books, Borrow published his tale of Bible-peddling in Spain. The book was a treasure for those who sought the thrills of vicarious adventuring. The fact that the traveler was far more often in the company of assassins, eccentric guides, romantic gypsies, and dangerous revolutionaries than in the company of Spain's aristocracy made it even more exciting. Readers must have felt, as some still do, that this travel book was written passionately out of a great experience. One event crowds upon another in a swiftly moving pageant of vivid scenes in town and country, the latter getting preference because of the author's love of the open road. One moves swiftly from lonely glen to wretched verminous hut; from wild storms at sea to rotting prisons in the hearts of great towns; from black nights on robber-infested roads to mountain villages which few foreigners had ever seen before.

Borrow remembers occasionally his solemn mission as an agent of the Bible Society, but his eagerness to convert the natives seems to be in exact proportion to the danger and difficulty of reaching them. His book is no thoughtful travel account. It exalts the sensational and bizarre at every turn of the road; it avoids poetry and dully factual reporting as if they were what Richard

Ford had told Borrow they were—equally plagues; and it gives itself to racing adventure.³ In almost every chapter the book motions its readers forward to a new group of characters with whom new adventures will take place. The book may leave one uncertain at a given moment whether its principal character, the traveler Borrow, is most like Don Quixote, Rousseau, Luther, or Defoe; but there is no doubt of the appeal of his travels. It is travel at its best. William Ernest Henley called it "as good a book about Spain as ever was written in any language." ⁴ George Saintsbury called it "one of the most brilliant and original books of travel ever written." ⁵ More recently, Hardin Craig called it Borrow's "most steadily interesting narrative." ⁶

But it was not merely because it was a travel account that Borrow's audience liked it. Much of its popularity came from their taking it to be an absolutely true narrative. Many of those who read it were people for whom the question, Is it Truth or is it merely Fiction? came with great moral significance. It would not have occurred to most of them that the truth of fiction may, upon occasion, transcend historical fact. They were not judging, as imaginative intellectuals, by Art; they appreciated Fact out of all proportion to its artistic importance. Undoubtedly, much of Borrow's success with his travel motif was because people accepted him as one hundred per cent truthful. They would have understood when Sherwood Anderson, nearly a century later, linked Borrow with Mark Twain because he sensed "the same quality of honesty in them." ⁷

Later there came to be doubts about the veracity of *The Bible in Spain*. William Dean Howells reflected the feeling when he said he thought Borrow's real tour was "filled in with invented incidents" so skillfully that Borrow might be considered "the master in this sort, so superlatively master as to seem sole in it after Defoe." ⁸ Arthur Compton-Rickett said later that he did not know whether Borrow should "go into the section devoted to novelists, or the section devoted to philosophers, or the section devoted to liars." ⁹ But no such suspicions clouded the minds of Borrow's early readers. They thought they had a true book of adventures, sanctified by a holy mission.

Believing that they were not wasting their time with idle fiction, Borrow's admirers could relish with quiet consciences another element in his treatment of the travel motif. This was the clearly discernible indebtedness to the picaresque tradition. It could not long have been a secret to any reader that, where other travel tales were usually informative but often dull, this man's books added a spice ordinarily reserved for pure fiction. Readers generally have found the deeds of a wandering rogue exciting, even when they could not approve of all of his roguery. But Borrow was a Christian *picaro,* a righteous rogue, one of those clever servants of God who appeared literally to fulfill the Gospel injunction to be as wise as serpents but as harmless as doves. Where had there been before in literature this union of dauntless missionary and complete *picaro?*

For Borrow *is* God's *picaro;* and, if he cheats anyone, it is the Pope. The Pope, of the Catholic world, is for him the traditional knavish "master" who must be undone by cleverness, by boldness, by whatever strategy the moment calls for. Borrow uses satire, invective, ridicule, faulty logic, and downright inaccuracies as he tilts against this recalcitrant windmill. And although the liberality which the *picaro* often exalts above everything else in his oft-victimized master (cf. Jack Wilton's joy when he locates Surrey in Thomas Nashe's *The Unfortunate Traveler*) is never credited to Romanism, a deliberate reversal may be seen in the praise Borrow gives his own religion. *It* is the generous, liberal master. The Pope is stingy, refusing education to his Spanish children. Protestantism gives generously in educating her children to the richer life (and, one is tempted to add, in providing adventurous missionaries with funds).

The *picaro* is usually interested in a profit; Borrow is, too, but it is God's profit. It is a curious arrangement—God will get the profit and the glory; Borrow will get the high adventure, the hiking and the fun. Borrow has the joys of divine sanction for his irresistible instinct for associating with the outcasts, Bohemians, and adventurous waifs of the world. Both in his life and in his writings, he clearly belongs to the great picaresque tradition.[10]

Borrow's readers could see how fully he met the requirements of this tradition or, where he failed, how he simply altered the customary motif to make the tradition acceptable. For example, Borrow meddled constantly in other people's affairs, even when he had no immediate objective to gain; and he did it as he did everything else—with the complete self-assurance, even impudence, of the true *picaro*. He moved with almost unbelievable ease from one level of society to another; he could talk with as much poise to Spain's prime minister as he had to a murderous villain on a mountain road. He was always ultimately successful, as one comes to expect the *picaro* to be; constantly in difficulty, he always just escaped death or disease or lifelong imprisonment; and he took it debonairly for granted that this would be. Above all, where the *picaro* was famous for tricking others and for living by his wits, Borrow made himself acceptable to his pious readers by employing these things unselfishly. He was not interested in tricking for food or money; he put his wits to work in a different way. Again and again he tricked people into accepting him as one of them, so that he might learn their ways and more successfully distribute Bibles among them, or, less altruistically, so that his insatiable appetite for languages might devour their dialect. His readers could chuckle heartily at a roguish trickster who was always a winner, and they could tell themselves that it was a pure laugh because their *picaro* tricked only for God.

There are other ways in which Borrow reflects the picaresque tradition. The *picaro*, for example, tells what he sees, without sentimentality. Borrow had learned to do this from his work in the compilation of the Newgate Calendar. His honest realism may be seen in dozens of passages like the description of the gypsy innkeepers of Tarifa in Chapter 4 of *Zincali*. Missionary though he was, he almost always refrains from preaching about the crimes and abuses which he sees. When Mrs. Herne, Jasper Petulengro's mother-in-law, tries to kill him, there follow no preachments upon that unsuccessful effort (*Lavengro*, II, 172-87 and 259-63). The *picaro* does not comment at length upon the Romantic aspects of nature; neither does Borrow, with two widely separated and apparently rather forced exceptions which will come up later in a discussion of his Romanticism. The *picaro* does not exhibit much direct human emotion, often appearing to be completely heartless. The total effect of reading Borrow is that he, too, is curiously detached. He may weep at a scene in nature in one of the exceptions noted above, but he does little weeping over men. He describes their plots and their personalities, makes the reader see them vividly; but he is objective, almost cold.

Like the *picaro*, Borrow lacked fear. This was not, as with Don Quixote, because he did not know the dangers inherent in a situation, but simply because he was supremely confident that his abilities and God's grace would see him through. The *picaro* feels no guilt; Borrow never betrays any dubiety about the tricks and stratagems he employed to accomplish his mission. The *picaro's* personality is generally static, the scene changes but the character (and those about him) remains the same. So it is with Borrow; we never feel that he is developing. He is presented with all his idiosyncrasies already a part of his tremendous self-confidence, and characters and events flow about him without denting his complacency.

In form, also, the picaresque motif prevails. Borrow's books have the episodic, loose structure of the genre. In his linear structure, the hero moves from place to place, and it is only his central figure which affords unity to the organization of the book. As the best recent study of the modes of fiction describes it: "In the picaresque novel, the chronological sequence is all there is: this happened and then that. The adventures, each an incident which might be an independent tale, are connected by the figure of the hero." [11] The structure of causation, which makes for a more philosophic novel, is almost completely lacking in Borrow, although he makes a weak attempt to interweave the characters of the old apple-woman, Benedict Mol, and some others in the largely plotless books.

That Borrow knew this picaresque tradition well is obvious from comments he makes as he records the Spanish adventures. Speaking of the Spanish aristocracy, he says: "Le Sage has described them as they were nearly two centuries ago. His description is anything but captivating, and I do not think that they have improved since the period of the sketches of the immortal Frenchman" (*The Bible in Spain*, I, 189). On another occasion, after describing the officious villains who came to take him to prison, he says that "Gil Blas, could he have waked from his sleep of two centuries, would, notwithstanding the change of fashion, have had no difficulty in recognizing them" (*The Bible*, II, 143). Elsewhere he calls Lazarillo de Tormes the father of the picaresque tradition and cites a minor tale of Cervantes as an amusing example of the genre (*Bible*, II, 296).

Frank Chandler, author of *The Literature of Roguery*, says that some of the tricks which Borrow describes in connection with jockeys are traceable to the picaresque narratives of Dekker and to *The English Rogue*.[12] However this may be, there are clear echoes of Le Sage. For example, where Le Sage got good effects by giving to Asmodeus the power to see through the roofs of houses, Borrow gets a similar effect by making his hero (himself) capable of reading thoughts or events more clearly than others (*Lavengro*, I, 27-28). One of his favorite tricks is to disconcert his companions by breaking through the façade of polite talk or false appearance to put his probing finger directly upon the real issue. Le Sage also has his hero often disguised to those among whom he moves, but plainly enough discerned by the audience, which knows that presently those who know him not will discover to their surprise a strange and powerful personality. So does it happen in Borrow's books, the little group in the tableau discovering at last that Don Jorge, or Lavengro, or Borrow is a truly great and wise man among them (*The Romany Rye*, I, 41). Then that particular episode ends, things become mundane again, and the traveler passes on to find other groups to mystify and enchant.

It is no wonder, then, that Borrow's books held such a fascination for those who liked to read of travel. The picaresque tradition is an exciting one, and Borrow employed many elements of the tradition skilfully. Augustine Birrell bears humorous witness to the exciting effects of Borrow's books. He remembers an invalid who put *The Bible in Spain* upon her counterpane, saying, "I feel as if I had been gesticulating violently for the space of two hours." The lady then sank into deep sleep and, according to Birrell, became hale and hearty.[13] Even the Borrovians must have winced at so partisan a witness, but it remains true that much of the fascination to be found in Borrow's books comes from the restless vagabondage so vividly portrayed in them.

One other strand was woven into Borrow's travel tales to their great credit in the eyes of English readers. In addition to being thought factual and racily picaresque, they were also seen to be ardently and vociferously nationalistic. Where that last great English wanderer, Lord Byron, had fled guiltily from his homeland

and hurled invective at her from a succession of European retreats, Borrow went boldly, with her full blessing, proclaiming loudly her superiority.

He believed that a man who could speak scornfully of his native land was capable of "the perpetration of any villainy, for, next to the love of God, the love of country is the best preventive of crime" (*The Bible*, I, 58). Even Catholicism, his arch enemy, is somewhat redeemed when it is embraced by Englishmen who love their native land. When Borrow meets some English Catholics in Lisbon, he is kinder to them than he has been to native communicants, calling their church an "ancient, grand, and imposing religion" and speaking of the believers as persons "full of amiability and courtesy to their heretic countrymen." He found them so patriotic that "even to the disparagement of those of their own darling faith" they stood up for England (*The Bible*, I, 69-71).

When a Portuguese military officer who accuses England of greed is tongue-lashed, Borrow apologizes for his action by saying: "I could not command myself when I heard my own glorious land traduced in this unmerited manner" (*The Bible*, I, 106-7). Spanish aristocrats are compared with their English counterparts to the former's great discredit: "Who can rival the English aristocrat in lofty stature, in dignified bearing, in strength of hand, and valour of heart?" He had posed this same question earlier in his account of the Spanish journeys, but his patriotic fervor here knows no bounds. "Who rides a nobler horse? Who has a firmer seat? And who more lovely than his wife, or sister, or daughter?" he asks triumphantly (*The Bible*, I, 189). All this admiration for the English aristocrat was to fade, but it was a heady ingredient in his most popular book.

Borrow even advises his older brother, aspiring to become a great painter, to find in incomparable England the inspiration he seeks as an artist (*Lavengro*, I, 228). England is the land of perfection; no charges against her are permitted to stand. When members of a Spanish political party spread, in talk and in print, a charge of bribery against the English government, Borrow laughs it off! "Such an accusation will of course merely extract a smile from those who are at all acquainted with the English character, and the general line of conduct pursued by the English government" (*The Bible*, I, 292).

A Bourgeois Byron

An unhappy Milanese with a "pale face and remarkably red nose" stands in a street of Coruña and tells Borrow that he would "rather be the poorest tramper on the roads of England than lord of all within ten leagues of the shore of the lake of Como." A little later the Italian speaks of "the green English hedgerows! and the ale-houses! and, what is much more, the fair dealing and security" (*The Bible*, I, 390, 393).

Finally, Borrow is always uncommonly moved when he thinks of England's military glory, or compares her soldiers with those of a foreign land. At Gibraltar, he carefully watches the sentries whose "bearing was that of British soldiers, conscious of the duties of their station. What a difference between them and the listless loiterers who stand at guard at the gate of a Spanish garrisoned town!" (*The Bible*, II, 326). His heart stirs at sight of Trafalgar, where a British force, "directed by one of the most remarkable men of the age, and perhaps the greatest hero of any time" defeated a far superior foe: "I never heard but one individual venture to say a word in disparagement of Nelson's glory: it was a pert American, who observed that the British admiral was much over-rated" (*The Bible*, II, 316).

No pious Evangelical Englishman, priding himself upon his preference for fact over fiction, or bravely admitting his taste for the picaresque, had any cause for regret when he sought these in Borrow's travel sections. And, when he also found upon the lips of this brave and holy English wanderer a constant hymn of nationalism, his joy must have been full.

II *Morality*

The fact that Borrow wrote travel tales containing three appealing ingredients is only one of the reasons for his great early success. A second major element in his books is the moralistic or religious note to be found there either in spoken platitudes or unspoken, but omnipresent, motivation for action. Modern readers tend to dislike this kind of thing; Victorians generally were fond of it. Students of literature soon come to recognize a climate of opinion which they call, loosely, "Victorian." In that climate, moralizing was in fashion. An author who turned aside from his narrative to deliver short sermons on morality and religion was not only not condemned, but liked the better for it. Today, wherever the popular audience still reads nineteenth-century novels with moralizing asides, it often simply skips what it calls "the preaching." Not so with Borrow's Evangelical readers; they found it one of the appealing elements in his books.

The word "conventional" is applied to these people and to their beliefs by almost every literary history of the period. They wanted their conclusions reaffirmed; they did not want to be shocked. Borrow must have seemed very safe to them, perhaps reminding them of Bunyan. Richard Ford said: "If the gypsy doctrine of Metempsychosis be true, the soul of honest John Bunyan has passed into the mortal coil of Mr. Borrow." He pointed out that Bunyan began as a tinker; gave it up for a sword, fighting with Cromwell; became a preacher and was imprisoned for it; and finally, in prison, turned author. Borrow, Ford says, followed a similar course, writing seriously during the time he was in prison at Madrid for his religious endeavors.[14]

The comparison is not far-fetched. The Methodist preacher, Peter Williams, not only sounds like Bunyan, but speaks very reverently of him (*Lavengro*, II, Ch. 73). And Borrow occasionally refers to Bunyan's masterpiece. For example, he says once when his horse sank in a bog: "This adventure brought to my recollection the meadow with its footpath which tempted Christian from the straight road to heaven, and finally conducted him to the dominions of the giant Despair" (*The Bible*, I, 350). Perhaps it is poetically just that these two titans, both bitterly critical of the Pope as a representative of the devil, should lie in graves only a stone's throw apart in Bunhill Fields, London.

But, if Borrow appeared to have Bunyan's earnestness, he did not have Bunyan's artistry. His moral and religious reflections are shallow. Doubtless this very quality, unrecognized as such, endeared him to his non-conformist audience. He said to them simply: "With respect to religious tenets, I wish to observe that I am a member of the Church of England, into whose communion I was baptized, and to which my forefathers belonged" (*Lavengro*, I, viii-ix). But everything he writes indicates that he was Low Church rather than High, and there is no indication that he knows or cares anything about what was called the Broad Church movement. Perceptive people saw then, as they have seen since, that most of his religious statements are "glib commonplaces of a man

who had found Christianity convenient, but not exactly sufficient." [15] Borrow wanted to travel, and the Bible Society gave
him a chance. He reciprocated by trumpeting every now and
then some religious sentiment.

When Borrow recalled the Spanish missionary effort, for example, he remembered it like this:

It is true that he went to Spain with the colors of that society on his
hat. Oh! the blood glows in his veins! oh! the marrow awakes in his old
bones when he thinks of what he accomplished in Spain in the cause
of religion and civilization with the colors of that society on his hat
and its weapon in his hand, even the sword of the Word of God; how
with that weapon he hewed left and right, making the priests fly before him, and run away squeaking: "Vaya! que demonio es este!"
                                    (*The Romany Rye*, II, 209)

One suspects that Borrow here reveals clearly how he really felt
about the more philosophical aspects of his mission. It was action
he wanted, not thought or meditation. When he begins to moralize or philosophize, he is superficial.

The superficiality reveals itself in at least four ways, all but one
of which would have been quite acceptable to his mass audience.
The one exception involves his strange inconsistencies of thought
and behavior, and was probably not clearly perceived by most of
his contemporary readers. The other three are his stereotyped language of piety, his prudery, and his lack of concern with the really
serious religious controversies of the time. But these weaknesses
reflect the tastes of his audience and helped secure his success.
They are, therefore, worth brief examination.

The conventional language which Borrow employs for his commonplace religious sentiments is found everywhere. At the end of
a perilous trip, during which there has been no intimation that
Borrow counted upon God for help, he pays his respects to Evangelical piety by saying: "After supper I went to bed, and, having
offered up my devotions to Him who had protected me through a
dangerous journey, I slept soundly till the morning" (*The Bible*, I,
34). Confronted by a stranger who was very brave in the day-
light, but became cowardly at night, Borrow recalled the events of
Acts 16 and said: "I now told him to call on the name of the Lord
Jesus, who was able to turn the darkness into light" (*The Bible*, I,

59). This statement seems contrived and out of tone with the personality Borrow has created. One senses that he remembers for whom he is writing and throws out periodically a sop. After much exciting adventure, during which the reader's thoughts have been directed toward Borrow's physical and mental prowess rather than toward God's power, comes this bow to religion: "Thus situated, like many other persons when human comfort is not at hand, I turned my thoughts to God, and began to commune with Him, the result of which was that my mind soon became quieted and comforted" (*The Bible,* I, 81-82).

The language Borrow uses for talking about his mission is often preachery, and it frequently conveys a kind of reverse boasting. Vowing that he intends to "ride forth, Testament in hand, and endeavour to circulate the Word of God" everywhere, he says:

I was aware that such a journey would be attended with considerable danger, and very possibly the fate of St. Stephen might overtake me; but does the man deserve the name of a follower of Christ who would shrink from danger of any kind in the cause of Him whom he calls his Master? 'He who loses his life for My sake shall find it,' are the words which the Lord Himself uttered. These words were fraught with consolation to me, as they doubtless are to everyone engaged in propagating the Gospel in sincerity of heart, in savage and barbarian lands.
(*The Bible* I, 278-79)

The connection with St. Stephen, the too-strongly-emphasized humility of the "can-I-do-less" argument, the citing of Scripture—these are all what any non-conformist churchgoer would expect to hear from his preacher or missionary. Since Borrow does not evince great interest in religion before or after the Spanish tours, the words ring hollow.

Borrow typically takes the Scripture which he quotes with extreme literalness. The subtleties of Christ's comment, "He who loses his life for my sake shall find it," probably escaped Borrow. He seems often to play with great religious ideas as if they were tamed and docile. Speaking once of Mr. Villiers, who when Borrow first arrived in Madrid was not well disposed towards the Bible Society, but later changed his mind, Borrow says glibly: "The holy Spirit had probably illumed his mind on this point"

(*The Bible*, I, 291). Since there is no evidence in any of his books
that he really felt strongly upon such matters, these remarks were
probably plucked from memories of church-going days and were
meant to reassure the Bible Society and his public as to his piety.

He says that he welcomes the chance to be imprisoned at Madrid as "a martyr, and as one suffering in the holy cause of religion," but a few hours later he admits to Villiers that he "was
under no apprehension whatever" about the final results! A little
later he decides to make the whole affair promote the glory of
England, without a word as to how it might serve the interests of
Christianity (*The Bible*, II, 141-42, 150-51). A few pages earlier,
he had already told his readers, in the customary religious manner, that he should not be cast down when things looked gloomi-
est, "as the hand of the Lord is generally then most busy: that
men may learn to perceive, that whatever good is accomplished is
not their work, but His" (*The Bible*, II, 78). But almost every
adventure Borrow has shows how quickly he could forget these
commonplace sentiments and rely rather upon his own strength
than upon God's.

Even upon a rare occasion when he momentarily probes
deeper, Borrow quickly hushes himself in the manner of the shallow religionist. Speaking of the people who were in the prison
with him at Madrid, he describes a strapping, dexterous house-
breaker who has his little son, dressed colorfully, upon his knee.
The criminal father dandles the child, sticks a cigar into its mouth
playfully, and exults in the way the prisoners pay court to the
infant. Puzzles Borrow: "What an enigma is this world of ours!
How dark and mysterious are the sources of what is called crime
and virtue! If that infant wretch become eventually a murderer
like his father, is he to blame? Fondled by robbers, already
dressed as a robber, born of a robber, whose own history was
perhaps similar. Is it right?" But he turns quickly away from the
dangers of such questioning and says to himself: "Oh, man, man,
seek not to dive into mystery of moral good and evil; confess
thyself a worm, cast thyself on the earth, and murmur with thy
lips in the dust, Jesus, Jesus!" (*The Bible*, II, 159-60).

Undoubtedly, the influence of the Bible Society lay upon much
of this writing. No matter how sincere Borrow may have been, his
"preachy" passages are now unsatisfactory. They employ the

pious language of the society, from which very real pressure was being exerted upon the exuberant colporteur.[16] His superiors insist upon conventionality; it is no surprise that, when he begins moralizing upon his mission, he turns to their diction. When he was questioned once about the limited number of Bibles he had circulated in Spain, he defended himself in language that clangs like hollow brass:

You say, 'There has not been much success in a week's work! Perhaps we only added one new recruit to the Society. One Bible sold in a week!' Who was that one recruit? 'Only a poor Spanish woman working the wine-press.' Now that is rather interesting. And maybe she had a large family, you say: five grown-up sons. [Borrow pauses, steps back, turns on the man, and in a loud voice that echoes up and down the street, says dramatically:] The mother of five sons added to the Church! Who can say where this great conquest will end? Who can say what was added to the Church when we added that peasant woman? Her sons may be five kings, five apostles, five statesmen. And you say only one recruit! Do you know who that one peasant woman is? When we added her to the Church we added a world! We added another flame—another invisible sun! [17]

This is a man in love with self-dramatization and rhetoric. We are not convinced of sincerity. Self-conscious and theatrical, almost all of Borrow's moralizing is marked by the stereotyped language of piety.

His morality is also prudish. This can be illustrated by his treatment of women, his comments upon wine, and his remark about the reading sins of his youth. A recent biographer, Martin Armstrong, makes much of "the total absence of the element of sexual love" in Borrow's novels.[18] After the excesses of Byron, Borrow represented the other extreme. And not only is this so, but, even when Borrow is only speaking of women, he uses a most cautious manner. Usually he simply calls them "females," but as the novels progress he sometimes concedes that they are "amiable" also. It comes as a surprise to find him speaking of a "very pretty female with a candle in her hand," or of an eldest daughter who was "remarkably handsome" (*The Bible*, II, 38; I, 380). But this is as far as he goes, and at times he is most painfully discreet, as in this passage: "We at last arrived nearly opposite to San Lucar, which stands at some distance from the water-side. Here a lively spectacle presented itself to us: the shore was covered with a multitude of females either dressing or undressing themselves, while (I speak within bounds) hundreds were in the water, sporting and playing" (*The Bible*, II, 297). It would appear that the implications of the word "lively" lingered upon Borrow's ear, embarrassing him into a parenthetical apology.

Once he refused to permit an old woman to kiss his cheek until he was assured that she wished to do so only because he reminded her of her only child, lost twenty years before at sea. "Oh," said Borrow, "that alters the case altogether, and of course I can have no objection" (*Lavengro*, I, 236).

At other times, he emphasizes his abstinence from strong drink. When an old Spanish curate offers it, Borrow writes: "We told him that we seldom drank ardent spirits; and I added, that as for myself, I seldom tasted even wine, but, like himself, was content with the use of water" (*The Bible*, I, 303). In a letter from Madrid to his mother he laments that the Spanish people do not resemble human beings because they "are almost as bad as the Irish, with the exception that they are not drunkards." [19]

Another indication of Borrow's superficiality in morality and philosophy appears in the inconsistencies which arise when he writes in this vein. Occasionally, some noticed that his professed love of humanity found no reflection at all in some of his other comments. An early reviewer linked with some of Borrow's expressions of piety his closing apostrophe to England, where he pleads with England to sink, if sink she must, "amidst blood and flame, with a mighty noise, causing more than one nation to participate in thy downfall." [20] But most people who read his books did not notice such discrepancies and considered him just as sincere as his admirer Theodore Watts-Dunton believed he was. [21]

The Bible Society objected to Borrow's speaking of his own good fortune; they preferred that he credit God's providence. He usually did what they wanted. Thus, in a precarious situation in the course of the Spanish tours, he says: "We of course expected to be robbed, perhaps stripped and otherwise ill-treated; but Providence here manifested itself" (*The Bible*, I, 271). Sometimes his crediting Providence properly leads him into a rather mechanical concept of God's over-riding care. He tells of entering La

Mancha, where he expected to fall into the hands of enemies, but "Providence again showed itself." The weather had been "delicious," but the Lord suddenly "breathed forth a frozen blast, the severity of which was almost intolerable." This godsend kept all the villains indoors while godly Borrow went about unharmed, but he admits that "the cold nearly killed us," Providence apparently having neglected to make the missionary's comfort complete.[22]

But at other times he forgets Providence altogether and simply credits chance. When he acquires Antonio, his remarkable and valuable servant, he says that "chance" brought him "at the very time I wanted him" (*The Bible*, I, 282). How the Bible Society employers must have winced at this neglect of an obvious opportunity to credit God with beneficent intervention in the affairs of their agent!

Borrow is equally inconsistent in the matter of humility. At times almost intolerably meek, he credits God with all his success and confesses that he is not yet completely Christian. "This answer of mine, I confess, was not that of a Christian, and proved to me how much of the leaven of the ancient man still pervaded me," he says, just after he has been insulting to an officer (*The Bible*, I, 106). "The Lord deigned to favour my feeble exertions in his cause at Lugo," he says elsewhere (*The Bible*, I, 378). But at other times, Borrow seems to glory in being cruel and merciless to someone who is not in a position to defend himself. Once, for example, he became so exasperated with a sluggish horse and its aged rider that he tied the bridle of the lazy animal to the crupper of his own horse, then

sparing neither spur nor cudgel, I soon forced my own horse into a kind of trot, which compelled the other to make some use of his legs. He twice attempted to fling himself down, to the great terror of his aged rider, who frequently entreated me to stop and permit him to dismount. I, however, took no notice of what he said, but continued spurring and cudgelling with unabated activity. (*The Bible*, I, 245-46)

These harsh sentiments contrast strikingly with Borrow's previous assertions of humility and meekness. But he could be even more truculent. Once he had some trouble with a man who wanted to be his guide. "I was now thoroughly incensed," he says, "and without a moment's reflection, spurred the jaca, which flung him down in the dust, and passed over him" (*The Bible*, II, 6).

He is equally inconsistent in other ways. He liked to think of himself as having the spirit of Christ and as eager to succor the benighted Spaniards. He tells how dangerous it is for him to scatter Testaments around Vargas, but he will not stop because he is eager to lay down his life for the cause (*The Bible*, II, 212). But he glories with equal fervor in his success as a cheat. Once, finding horses scarce in his locality, he sold his own horse at a far higher price than the animal had cost, then boasted: "I was glad to part with him for more reasons than one; he was both vicious and savage, and was continually getting me into scrapes in the stables of the posadas where we slept or baited." A little later he learned that the horse he sold "became glandered and died." "Peace to his memory!" he says blithely (*The Bible*, II, 44-45).

He praised the Bible as warmly as an Evangelical reader could have wished. It is, he says to a village schoolteacher in Portugal, "calculated . . . of itself to illume the minds of all classes of mankind" (*The Bible*, I, 11-12). It is, he says to one Don Geronimo in Evora, "the well-head of all that is useful and conducive to the happiness of society" (*The Bible*, I, 42). But he records what may have been a truer statement of his unemployed attitude when he cites another's belief that its philosophy is unsound. William Taylor, his Norwich philosopher-friend, called the Bible "respectable," but added that he should "hardly call it one whose philosophy is of the soundest." It has too much passion and violence; it is not cool and dispassionate enough, he argues. Borrow does not challenge this statement (*Lavengro*, I, 246).

It is hard to believe, in view of these waverings, that Borrow was anything other than superficial in his moralizing. It would appear that he recalled his status as agent of the Bible Society at certain moments, and spoke befittingly; while at others, caught up in the spirit of adventure and glowing with self-confidence, he forgot his obligations and spoke more honestly.

The shallowness of Borrow's approach to religion is revealed again in his almost complete lack of concern with the deeper religious controversies of his time. The audience he wrote for was large and influential, and it was not much interested in the profunditions of religious debate. There is no serious attempt in his books to grapple with the problems suggested by the three great divisions within the Anglican fold: Evangelical, High Church, and the small but vocal Broad Church minority. For the Evangelicals, he had only a repetition, in trite phrases, of their dogma. Of the High Church, with its loyalty to the older rituals and customs, he had little to say. And the Broad Church element was doubtless too intellectual for him to understand completely. Not really a separate body, but rather a very liberal party within the High Church, this group was interested in the new Biblical criticism of the Tübingen school in Germany. But Borrow took refuge in the Evangelical tradition and simply refused to permit himself the privilege of speculation.

Oddly, although the famed Tract XC of the *Tracts for the Times* of the Oxford Movement was issued in 1841, when Borrow was working on *The Bible in Spain,* he does not use this contemporary illustration of the dangers of Catholicism in his fight against the Roman religion. Newman's final step into Catholicism in 1845 probably influenced the increasing viciousness with which Borrow attacked Rome, but even in *Lavengro* and in *The Romany Rye* there is no specific, thoughtful discussion of the issues, but only calumny and abuse.

Borrow's lack of depth in consideration of religious issues is also apparent in his failure to pay any attention to the doctrine of evolution. Erasmus Darwin, Chevalier de Lamarck, George Cuvier and Sir Charles Lyell were preparing the way for Charles Darwin years before the publication of *The Bible in Spain.* Yet Borrow, who poses as a champion of true religion, nowhere gives any hint that he saw this great conflict shaping up. Some of the famous *Bridgewater Treatises,* composed to combat the theory of evolution, were already written before Borrow published his first book; but he seemed unaware of them.

This neglect of the important issues by one who poses as God's champion somewhat repels readers now. But Borrow's nonconformist audience probably felt that he had done the right thing. No matter what the cost, it preferred the security of feeling that it was holding fast to the traditions of its fathers. His audiences wanted no new and disturbing ideas set abuzzing in their heads. Borrow rubber-stamps their opinions and makes them happy; he had learned early just how important an ingredient this element of conventional moralizing can be in successful books.

The lesson came in this manner: Borrow's first hesitant offerings to the world of letters were some old ballads and a romance. The London publisher to whom he presented them told him that readers were not interested in that sort of thing, and he gave Borrow some advice. As dramatized by Borrow, the incident went as follows:

"Don't you think you could write a series of Evangelical tales?" said the publisher.

"Evangelical tales, sir?"

"Yes, sir, evangelical novels . . . something in the style of the *Dairyman's Daughter.*"

"I never heard of the work till the present moment."

"Then, sir, procure it by all means. Sir, I could afford as much as ten pounds for a well-written tale in the style of the *Dairyman's Daughter;* that is the kind of literature, sir, that sells at the present day." (*Lavengro*, I, 315)

Undoubtedly, much of the shallow moralizing in Borrow's popular books was the result of this insight into public taste. *The Dairyman's Daughter* had been written by an Evangelical clergyman, Mr. Leigh Richmond, and was enormously popular.[23]

When Borrow, in response to his publisher's suggestion, went into a bookstore to buy the book, a conversation ensued in the course of which he asked the bookseller: "Who are the Evangelical party?" The bookseller told him gravely that they were "religious, good men." Asked Borrow: "Not a set of canting scoundrels?" The bookseller told him solemnly that he had better leave the shop. But Borrow soothed him and tricked the man into giving him the book. This incident has the ring of truth and probably represents how Borrow really felt about the folk of Earl Street (*Lavengro*, I, 329-30). But when he got the chance to visit Spain, expenses paid, it may not have been hard for a flexible mind to forget such sentiments and to pay lip-service to Evangelical piety.

There were scornful laughs by some who had known Borrow before his connection with the Bible Society, but he explained his conversion smoothly and made his bow toward Evangelical professions of humility.[24] He knew that his age was "an age of humbug, in which everything to obtain much note and reputation must depend less upon its own intrinsic merits than on the name it bears" (*The Bible*, II, 432); so in a stroke of genius, he became an agent of the Bible Society and named his one really successful book *The Bible in Spain*, a title which can appropriately be used of only about one-fiftieth of the contents.

III   *Flamboyant Personality*

The third ingredient in Borrow's books, which could hardly have been less appealing than the travel narratives and the moralizing, was stamped upon every page: the mark of a unique personality. The word "flamboyant" suggests the quality of a personality that is superficial and flashy. Wherever one looks into his books, Borrow's personality dazzles him.

Here again, some of Borrow's first readers must have been reminded of Byron, dead a generation before. There is much the same pre-occupation with self, with that measure of egotism which is so supreme that it becomes almost a virtue; there is the same self-conscious and deliberately cultivated air of mystery and romance; there is the same occasional melancholia, heightened by contrast with the prevailing tone of extreme self-confidence; and there is the same intense focusing of hatred upon a self-chosen foe.[25]

In other ways, Borrow was clearly unlike Byron. There is no hint of any personal interest in sexual pleasures. The Isopel Berners episode has been mentioned. In addition, there was the long talk with pretty Ursula Petulengro under the thorn hedge, so fraught with sensual excitement on her part, but so cool a thing with the righteous Borrow (*The Romany Rye*, I, 97-115), and the similar talk with an Irish girl in the closing chapters of *Wild Wales* (II, 438-49). These situations end rather frustratingly for the modern reader, not because Borrow has not responded to the excitement, but because he has not even seemed to be aware of it. But, for those who were ready to react against Byronism, it must have been satisfying. Borrow's caution about wine and his great care never to offend in matters of profanity and blasphemy were probably equally pleasing.

In the compound of personality traits which makes up the flamboyant Borrow, there are four principal elements. Each one may be illustrated upon almost any page of his novels, although most completely in the popular Spanish tour account. Combined, they create so lasting an impression of an eccentric that to this day those who know Borrow at all are more likely to recall his personal quaintness than the quality of his writings.

The most memorable trait in Borrow's makeup is his love of gypsy life. At a certain level of literacy, one may ask who George Borrow was and obtain repeatedly the same answer: "Oh, he was the gypsy man, wasn't he?" The respondent means, not only that Borrow wrote about gypsies, but that he remains in the memory as something of a gypsy himself.

Borrow talked much of his interest, as a linguist, in the odd language of the gypsies and of his curiosity about their customs and traditions. But his interest was much more personal than that. He liked their free mode of life, their healthy journeyings upon the windy heath, their powerfully loyal clannishness. He knew that they were often cheats, liars, and thieves; but they fascinated him no less. Any reader of his books finds that Borrow is most completely himself when in the company of his gypsy friends. There, and only there, he loses the self-conscious restraint that characterizes his conduct when he is with his social equals or superiors. Jasper Petulengro, Borrow's epitome of gypsyism, is perhaps Borrow's true aristocrat; Isopel Berners is certainly the most attractive woman he ever met.

By temperament, Borrow is a gypsy himself. He likes to describe himself, and many other objects, in their language. The exotic words cast a spell over some of the most ordinary subjects. He has the gypsy love of carefree movement, the insatiable appetite for new places and new thrills. The one thing he cannot abide is routine.[26]

It is no surprise, therefore, that his first major literary effort was an account of the gypsies of Spain. He confesses in the first paragraph of that book that he "can remember no period when the mentioning of the name of Gypsy did not awaken feelings within [his] mind hard to be described, but in which a strange pleasure predominated" (*Zincali*, pp. 1, 32). *Lavengro* and *The Romany Rye* do not belie their gypsy titles; they are filled with some of the most memorable sketches of gypsy life ever written.

The Gypsy Lore Society has an elaborate bibliography of works on the origin, history, customs, institutions, and languages of the gypsies. Many surpass as purely factual studies anything Borrow wrote. But, as Theodore Watts-Dunton did in his novel *Aylwin,* they emphasize literalness so strongly that what the average man believes to be the essential qualities of the gypsy—mystery and romance—are lost. Borrow did not make this mistake; it is he, consequently, who is remembered as "the gypsy man."

Another element in Borrow's personality is his amazing self-confidence. Like Whitman, he sings himself. "He is . . . a colossal egotist who in his journeyings takes up the whole road." [27] He so masters the mind of the reader that inconsistencies and stylistic defects are scarcely noticed. Writing in the first person, he is superbly confident, invariably successful in every crisis. Both physically and mentally he towers above his companions in whatever land he finds himself.

Physically, Borrow had every reason to be self-assured. Friends and acquaintances remember him as an almost perfect specimen, tall, powerfully built, and handsome. Watts-Dunton says he "had a countenance of extraordinary impressiveness, if not of commanding beauty—Greek in type with a dash of Hebrew," adding that "there had never before appeared on the English highroads so majestic looking a tramp." [28] John Gibson Lockhart described him as "tall, strong, athletic, with a clear olive complexion, and eyes full of the fire of genius and enterprise, his hair already white as Mont Blanc." [29] A. Egmont Hake told how he and Borrow one day in March walked through Richmond Park in a bitterly cold wind and came to the Fen Ponds, which had ice on them: "Borrow stripped and jumped into the water, diving for a long distance and reappearing at a far-off spot. He was then seventy years of age." [30] Watts-Dunton compared Borrow favorably with E. J. Trelawny, Shelley's vigorous old friend; but he also says that "at seventy Borrow could have walked off with Trelawny under his arm." [31]

The *Bury Post* in 1853 related how Borrow saved one man from raging surf and helped save others.[32] But perhaps the most interesting testimonial is one given by Elizabeth Barrett. Writing to her friend Mary Mitford, she said in 1843:

Mr. Kenyon was at Mr. Chorley's the other evening, and from thence went to Mr. Babbages' where he met among divers notabilities, Mr. Borrow the Gypsey. You know, or you ought as soon as possible to know, Borrow's 'Bible in Spain' and 'Gypsies in Spain.' He is full of Genius—you may *almost* call it genius, ... Mr. Kenyon says that he looked 'every inch a' . . . *man,* as he stood in Mr. Babbages draw-ing-room, . . . with six feet three of height, bone and muscle, . . . grey large earnest eyes, aquiline nose, determined mouth,—fit to be the lion he was! [33]

In a later letter she characterized Borrow as "a Dare-all," saying she liked him "all the better for putting off the conventional de-mureness of a pattern missionary, and daring to be a *man* 'in spirit and in truth.'" [34]

Borrow had no reluctance about presenting himself as a man who gloried in physical prowess and who recommended an active, outdoor life for others. He said that he found out early in life what the world would offer him, and how he could conquer it. On his way to London after his father's death, a conman shouted to him: "One-and-ninepence, sir, or your things will be taken away from you!" Borrow clenched his fists, and the man faltered. Mused Bor-row: "Am I to expect many of these greetings in the big world? Well, never mind: I think I know the countersign!" (*Lavengro,* I, 303).

When he went to London in December, 1832, for his first meet-ing with the Bible Society, he walked one hundred twelve miles. Too poor to hire a carriage or ride in a coach, he spent only five-pence half-penny on the trip, purchasing a pint of ale, a half pint of milk, a roll of bread, and two apples. The trip took slightly more than twenty-seven hours.

In his books, Borrow continually presents himself as unusually strong, agile, and durable. He tells of spending an entire night in a forest with cold, drizzling rain falling: "The sun was just appear-ing as I awoke. I made several efforts before I could rise from the ground; my limbs were quite stiff, and my hair was covered with rime" (*The Bible,* I, 145-46). One of his villainous acquaintances once unsheathed a "snick and snee" knife and would have cut another man open "had I not pulled his arm down just in time to prevent worse effects than a scratch above the lower jawbone," says Borrow (*The Bible,* I, 98). Some who traveled with him on dark, dangerous roads were fearful; but Borrow says that "the dangers of the night daunt [him] no more than those of midday" (*The Bible,* I, 60). He frets under the physical inactivity imposed by the writer's tasks. "What a contemptible trade is an Author's compared with that of a jockey," he says to his publisher.[35] He watches a group of "fine lads, sporting in a court below" his window at Lisbon and says: "This is as it should be . . . those boys will not make worse priests from a little early devotion to trap-ball and cudgel playing" (*The Bible,* I, 72).

Mentally, Borrow had perhaps less reason for boasting, but he was not deterred. Whenever he is humorous, it is almost always the result of situations in which he has been the master, the *picaro,* tricking someone by clever use of his wits. He fancied himself in possession of strange supernatural powers. He tells how a Jewish peddler called at his parents' home when he was still a lad and saw him to be a child of genius. After saying to the maid that it was not his custom to speak to children, the peddler admits that he had "no sooner looked at that child" [Borrow] than he "was forced to speak to it . . . a prophet's child." A moment later, the Jew looked at some lines which the child Borrow had traced in the dust. His reaction is a tribute to the innate powers Borrow would like his readers to believe he possessed: "All of a sudden he started back, and grew white as a sheet; then, taking off his hat, he made some strange gestures to me, cringing, chattering, and showing his teeth, and shortly departed, muttering something about 'holy letters,' and talking to himself in a strange tongue" (*Lavengro,* I, 12-13).

Soon after this, Borrow tells the story of the beautiful but poisonous viper which menaced his brother, but made no effort to harm him, even while he held it in his hand. He said it was his "firm belief that certain individuals possess an inherent power, or fascination, over certain creatures, otherwise I should be unable to account for many feats which I have witnessed, and, indeed, borne a share in, connected with the taming of brutes and reptiles" (*Lavengro,* I, 15-16).

Borrow also reveled in his linguistic talents. There is no self-consciousness about the following typical comment: "And, being already acquainted with most of the principal languages and dia-

[64]

lects of the east and the west, I am soon able to make myself quite intelligible to the inhabitants. In about a fortnight I found myself conversing in Portuguese with considerable fluency" (*The Bible,* I, 4).

He once put a book before a friend, Elizabeth Harvey, and, when she could not read it, told her it was in her own language, Saxon. But when another person tried such a trick on him, he objected: "What's that, trying to come over me with strange languages." [36] The titles of his books reflect this affectation. Lavengro means "word-master"; Romany Rye means "gypsy gentleman." Borrow is willing at any time to interrupt a narrative in favor of a dissertation on linguistics. A chapter in *The Bible in Spain* is devoted to the origin and peculiarities of the Basque language, the Sanskrit and Tartar dialects (II, Ch. 37). Borrow likes to tell how he dazzled natives. An old man in Spain is amazed that Protestant Borrow should "understand the language of the church" and says: "Vaya! The longer one lives the more one learns" (*The Bible,* I, 261).

The biographers tend generally to accept Borrow's faith in his linguistic abilities. Herbert Jenkins, who affirms that Borrow was familiar with forty-one languages, lists them all.[37] Clement Shorter testifies that he could read and speak a great many.[38] William I. Knapp also credits Borrow with great facility in languages, but he points out that Borrow often made mistakes. Knapp says that the word "Zincali" was improperly used by Borrow in the title of his first book, since it would signify a gypsy female if it were ever used at all.[39] Borrow, of course, used the word as a plural. And David Salmon, writing a brief note on Borrow's Welsh, says: "His apprehension of the meaning of any text [Borrow had translated Welsh songs] was not exact; when he tried to speak, his words were literary rather than colloquial, his mutations were generally wrong, and his pronunciation was outlandish." [40] But such voices were rare in Borrow's own time, and he brushed off detractors with great confidence. He believed in himself with such ardor that cults of Borrovians sprang up in his wake.

Another element of Borrow's strange personality was his fanatical and unreasoning hatred of Catholicism. He was a good hater without regard to the object, but his absolute antipathy toward anything resembling Catholicism was impressive. The attack never ceases for long in his books. In the Preface to *The Bible in Spain*, a book which naturally lent itself to almost continuous criticism of Catholicism, he speaks of the "spiritual tyranny of the court of Rome"; of Spain as "the she-butcher, La Verduga, of malignant Rome, the chosen instrument for carrying into effect the atrocious projects of that power"; of Spain "ceasing to be the butcher" and becoming instead "the banker of Rome"; of the Pope as "Batuschca," who ought to "undeceive himself" because Spain was no longer ready to fight for him; and of his belief that two English missionaries, had they not been banished, might have caused many thousands in Spain to discard "forever the last relics of Popish superstition" (*The Bible*, I, xx, xxi, xxiii, xxvi).

He doubted that Romanism was kinder than in the days of the Inquisition. On his way to prison in Madrid, remembering that once he would have been burned, he says: "Pope of Rome! I believe you to be as malicious as ever, but you are sadly deficient in power. You are become paralytic, Batuschca, and your club has degenerated to a crutch" (*The Bible*, II, 146). At a Moorish mosque, he says:

I looked around for the abominable thing, and found it not; no scarlet strumpet with a crown of false gold sat nursing an ugly changeling in a niche. "Come here," said I, "Papist, and take a lesson; here is a house of God, in externals at least, such as a house of God should be; four walls, a fountain, and the eternal firmament above, which mirrors His glory. . . . Fool, thy walls are stuck with idols; thou callest a stone thy Father, and a piece of rotting wood the Queen of Heaven."

(*The Bible*, II, 379)

In his later books, he is no better. He says in *Lavengro* that he is disgusted with these times of "universal tolerism," and in *The Romany Rye* he gives himself almost irrationally to the most virulent descriptions of Catholicism in the Man in Black episodes.

He was probably sincere about it. As late as 1924 he had apologists. The *Times Literary Supplement* pointed out that Borrow had no reason to think well of priests, having spent years among the most backward peasants in western Europe in the service of a society which held passionately to a Protestant theory about the saving power of The Word. But however sincere Borrow may have been, his conviction that he challenged Catholicism in a lucid, reasonable manner shakes one's faith in his judgment. In the Appendix to *The Romany Rye*, he says of his book that "perhaps no work was ever offered to the public in which . . . the machinations of priestcraft have been more truly and lucidly exposed" (II, 194). He refers particularly to the Man in Black episodes in the first of that book. But they are outrageously contrived and superficial, the outpourings of a vindictive, bitter man. There is excellent dialogue (Borrow wrote well when he was hating) and some racy narration, but to call this trivial account of Catholicism "true" or "lucid" seems preposterous to most readers. Sherwood Anderson once advised a friend to read Borrow for his stylistic merits, but said: "I warn you, Paul, the damn old cuss is a nut on the church, always putting it in the worst possible light." [41]

Borrow's hatred was so intense that he was doubtless unaware of the inconsistencies which pro-Catholic writers have since pointed out in his books. Owen B. McGuire says that Borrow praises very highly certain qualities in the Spanish people which could not possibly have existed had they been so enslaved and degraded by the Roman church as Borrow makes them out.[42] And a writer for the *Dublin Review* said in 1914: "It is not difficult to find a certain jovial duplicity in his theory and practice. He was ever ready to abuse Popery, but his praise of the different priests who became his friends and hosts makes a curious commentary within his own book." [43]

But in spite of such criticism, there seems little doubt that Borrow's Evangelical audience was inclined to like a personality which could feel so strongly about its arch-foe. A measure of the strength of its admiration may be found in the violent denunciation of Borrow by the *Edinburgh Review*:

Mr. Borrow, then, is a missionary—a missionary sent out by a gang of conspirators against Christianity, who denominate themselves the Bible Society; whose headquarters are, we believe, fixed in London, and who live and carry on their operations at the expense of some thousands of persons, who are dupes, or knaves enough to spend their money in supporting a swarm of vagabonds, trampers, incendiaries, and hypocrites, in every quarter of the globe.[44]

In such an atmosphere, Borrow's own virulence can be better understood; and this evidence shows that his intense, blind, and unflagging hatred of Catholicism was a salient ingredient in the excitement his personality held for ardent Protestants. If, as it will appear later, one of Borrow's reasons for pre-empting a Biblical style unique in its fullness was so that he might show how close he was to "The Book" as an enlightened Protestant, then every Biblical rhythm and allusion served as a constant reminder that a Catholic-hating Bible-reader was speaking.

Finally, there is in Borrow's bizarre makeup a whole set of contradictions. We have seen already how inconsistent he is with reference to his treatment of morality and religion, but the inconsistency pervades his entire personality. He so completely misjudges himself as to say that he is "neither fiery, enthusiastic nor openhearted" and is fond of "study and reflection" (*The Bible*, I, 210). In a melting mood he can forget his usual aversion to sentimentality and burst into profuse tears. Lying upon a hill above the Tweed River, he is overcome by the beauty of "the prospect" and says, "my bosom began to heave and my tears to trickle" (*Lavengro*, I, 71).

He frequently boasts of his natural gentility. The servant of a rich old English gentleman spoke to him condescendingly as he looked at his shoes, but said, "I beg your pardon, sir" as he looked Borrow in the face (*Lavengro*, I, 255). But he can be quite boorish, causing considerable embarrassment by his rudeness. One of his biographers cites this example:

Once his hostess, a simple unpretending woman desirous only of pleasing her distinguished guest, said, "Oh, Mr. Borrow, I have read your books with so much pleasure!" "Pray, what books do you mean, madam? Do you mean my account books?" was the ungracious retort. He then rose from the table, fretting and fuming and walked up and down the dining-room among the servants . . . till the carriage could be ordered for our return home.[45]

He thinks of himself as a man completely in control of his faculties, but he has also to confess occasional madness and loss of consciousness of identity. At one point, in *Lavengro*, he recounts such an occurrence in vivid language: "Suddenly I started up, and could scarcely repress the shriek which was rising to my lips. Was it possible? Yes, all too certain; the evil one was upon me; the inscrutable horror which I had felt in my boyhood had once more taken possession of me" (*Lavengro,* II, 284). The passage, which goes on at some length, describes the seizure as "the screaming horror." It is, throughout, a powerfully written portrait of a man fighting stark terror.

All these quirks of personality promoted high public interest in Borrow. Some readers are always eager to turn to a book when they hear that the author is "odd." In Borrow's case, they were not disappointed, and what they found led many of them to consider themselves ever afterwards as "Borrovians." As Augustine Birrell, one of them, said: "His personality will always secure him an attendant company, who, when he pipes, must dance." [46] Birrell, indeed, seems to have been the first to use the phrase "Borrovian Cult" in describing these admirers. They had an interesting, if short-lived, history.[47]

The preceding pages have attempted to show that Borrow's popularity with the Evangelical public of the mid-nineteenth century was inevitable since he provided them with the very things they wanted from a hero novelist: travel tales, conventional morality, and the impress upon every page of one of the most startling personalities English literature has ever known. How these elements were reflected in stylistic techniques is the subject of the next section.

CHAPTER 3

The Craftsman

IT IS possible to distinguish several prose styles in Borrow's books. He may move abruptly from a colloquial style in his vivid travel sections to a heavily ornate and artificial style which he seems to consider appropriate for his philosophical moods. Or he may turn suddenly from his usual restrained and realistic technique of description to momentary dalliance with Romanticism—meaning, in his case, excessive idealization of rural life, a strange use of fancy in some bits of description, and sentimental melancholy.

Nineteenth- and early twentieth-century criticism of Borrow's style was imprecise. Eulogistic critics called his prose simple, plain, powerful, vigorously alive, racy and used all the complimentary phrases which compose the vocabulary of impressionistic criticism. W. E. Henley called Borrow's style "racy, nervous, idiomatic English, with a kind of eloquence at once primitive and scholarly, precious but homely. . . ." [1] George Saintsbury judged Borrow the "superior of both [Defoe and Dumas] in pure style and in the literary quality of his work." [2] Sherwood Anderson confessed to being a long-time Borrow fan and said: "The old bastard is, I fear, a complete fraud, but he can write, and I love his flamboyancy and gush." [3] Arthur Conan Doyle, who once parodied Borrow's style marvelously, apologized for that amiable impudence in these words: "But, my word, what English the fellow could write! What an organ-roll he could get into his sentences! How nervous and vital and vivid it all is! There is music in every line of it if you have been blessed with an ear for the music of prose." [4] As late as 1938, a critic spoke of Borrow's prose as having "the qualities of a clear mountain stream rushing cleanly and precipitously along," but approached more analytical criticism by speaking of "archaic phrasings" and "inordinate apostrophes." [5]

In view of such eulogies, however imprecise, one may wonder whether Borrow himself was self-conscious about prose style. Some of his readers accepted Buffon's dictum, "Le style, c'est l'homme," rather too literally and saw Borrow's style as a kind of innate inheritance. One of them called Borrow a writer "in spite of himself." [6] But a London *Times* book reviewer made much more sense:

Borrow had theories about most things, and it is only reasonable to suppose that he had theories about style. Artists do not blunder into beauty; and great triumphs of the pen, as of the sword, are not produced without an infinity of pains and thought, and an infinity of delight in production. Borrow was a very great artist. He was not a man "to fling whate'er he felt, not fearing, into words." [7]

John Macy credited Borrow with the ability to achieve fascinating stylistic effects by varying with his "short arm jab or his over-hand wallop." [8]

Borrow's own comments indicate that he was aware of the literary influences and arduous training that lie behind the formation of a good prose style. His two most significant statements are both in *Lavengro*. In the first, he acknowledges Defoe as a model, praises him extravagantly, and apostrophizes: "Hail to thee, spirit of DeFoe! What does not my own poor self owe to thee?" (I, 32). In the second, he confesses that of all his early drudgeries in London, he liked best that of compiling the *Newgate Lives and Trials*. He liked the "racy, genuine language" and "the art which the writers, whoever they were, possessed of telling a plain story" (I, 361).

He quotes an illustrative sentence from the *Lives:* "So I went with them to a music booth, where they made me almost drunk with gin, and began to talk their flash language, which I did not understand." Then he says: "I have always looked upon this sentence as a masterpiece of the narrative style, it is so concise and yet so very clear" (*Lavengro,* I, 361-62). It is not surprising that almost every critic who discussed Borrow's merits in the nineteenth century should have discovered these very qualities in his best work. It is true that Borrow occasionally tried too hard to impress his readers, at which times his style invariably deteriorated. But at his finest he captures the clarity and simplicity which he coveted.

I *The Story-Teller*

Borrow wisely chose to write colloquially when he related his adventures. The plainness of his style contrasts vividly with the lush prose of most of the adventure stories of his contemporaries. Since most of the typical ones are no longer easily available, extracts may be helpful. Here is one from a travel narrative published three months before Borrow's story of his Spanish adventures:

Crashing through bushes in their fall, and rebounding from rock to rock, the noble steeds struggled madly to dash their feet into the soil and stop their downward course—but all in vain. With nostrils wide distended, and blood pouring from every limb, they toiled and wrestled with their fate. The deep abyss swallowed them up; and the wild vulture, scenting his carrion from afar, floated madly downward from the topmost peak of the mountain, from which he had been a spectator of their fate. His talons were fixed in the still quivering flank of one of the horses, which turned its dying eyes in terror on its ruthless destroyer; but, with a hoarse croak, the vulture darted his beak into the maddened charger's side, and a moment of fearful agony put an end to its woes forever.[9]

Every sentence is over-written. The writer is particularly enamored of "madly" and "maddened." Sentimentalism runs riot. Beside this hysterical rhetoric we may place the description of an exciting moment in Borrow's Spanish tour:

Only a quarter of an hour previous I had passed three ghastly heads stuck on poles standing by the wayside; they were those of a captain of banditti and two of his accomplices, who had been seized and executed about two months before. Their principal haunt was the vicinity of the bridge, and it was their practice to cast the bodies of the murdered into the deep black water which runs rapidly beneath. Those three heads will always live in my remembrance, particularly that of the captain, which stood on a higher pole than the other two: the long hair was waving in the wind, and the blackened, distorted features were grinning in the sun. (*The Bible*, I, 383-84)

In this restrained telling, with precise location of the spot lending veri-similitude, Borrow permits himself only one emotional adjective, "ghastly"; and it proves, as one reads on, to be a rather restrained description of what any modern reader would think horrible. There is no hysteria or sentimentalism, although the episode could easily call for both.

Theodore Watts-Dunton admired Borrow greatly and was influenced by him. But he was unable to throw off the taste of the times; and, not long after Borrow had stopped writing altogether, Watts-Dunton composed *Aylwin,* a novel whose gypsy lore indisputably connects it with Borrow. Here is Watts-Dunton in a sentimental mood:

A mist of cruel trouble was covering his eyes, and soon the mist had grown into two bright glittering pearly tears, which, globing and trembling, larger and larger, were at length big enough to drown both eyes; big enough to drop, shining, on the grass; big enough to blot out altogether the most brilliant picture that sea and sky could make. For that little boy had begun to learn a lesson which life was going to teach him fully—the lesson that shining sails in the sunny wind, and black trailing bands of smoke passing here and there along the horizon, and silvery gulls dipping playfully into the green and silver waves (nay, all the beauties and all the wonders of the world), make but a blurred picture to eyes that look through the lens of tears.[10]

Borrow, at a time when he might have been similarly lachrymose, describes the final departure from Isopel Berners in this simple, restrained way:

On arriving at the extremity of the plain, I looked towards the dingle. Isopel Berners stood at the mouth; the beams of the early morning sun shone full on her noble face and figure. I waved my hand towards her. She slowly lifted up her right arm. I turned away, and never saw Isopel Berners again. (*Romany Rye,* I, 154)

Such writing must have been an interesting novelty for many of Borrow's readers. It explains why critics invariably spoke of his naturalness, his forthrightness, his refusal to employ super-eloquence.

Two Victorians, themselves novelists and acquainted with the difficulties of rising above the high-flown rhetoric and sentimentalism of their times, praise Borrow's plain style. Charlotte Brontë commends his "athletic simplicity," and J. H. Shorthouse calls Borrow's language "perfectly simple, plain, and unaffected," adding that its style "is, by its delightful simplicity, a refreshment in the turmoil and confusion of the world of letters of the present day." [11]

It is interesting to compare Borrow's opening words in *The Bible in Spain* with those of Théophile Gautier, who was in Spain at the same time Borrow was and who later wrote an account of that visit. Gautier's original version lacks the virility of Borrow's account, although it is not so stiff and dry as the English translation: "So on the 5th of May I proceeded to rid my country of my importunate person, and climbed into the Bordeaux stagecoach, which took me to that city and Bayonne, where we took the Madrid coach, in which we reached the Bidassao River." [12] Borrow's opening words are more spirited and lively: "On the morning of the 10th of November, 1835, I found myself off the coast of Galicia, whose lofty mountains, gilded by the rising sun, presented a magnificent appearance. I was bound for Lisbon; we passed Cape Finisterre, and, standing farther out to sea, speedily lost sight of land" (*The Bible*, I, 1). Borrow launches immediately into an exciting adventure which captures the spirit of mystery and daring at the same time.

Another comparison between the two accounts involves the only mutual acquaintance the two travel writers had, the famed bull-fighter Sevilla. Describing the champion as he looked in the Madrid arena, Gautier calls him "a robust Hercules, with superb eyes and the physiognomy of one of Titian's Caesars, with an expression of jovial and contemptful serenity. . . ." [13] Borrow saw quite a different man. In a vicious tavern—"a low tavern in a neighborhood notorious for robbery and murder"—he was accosted by "a horrible-looking fellow, with a white hat with a rim a yard and a half in circumference, dressed in a buff jerkin, leather breeches and jack boots." After learning that Borrow could speak prison slang, this person made much of him, stood him drink, and bore loud public testimony to him, saying: "He is a good ginete, too; next to myself, there is none like him, only he rides with stirrup leathers too short." The episode ends with the man's beating his breast and shouting, "Io Sevilla!" (*The Bible*, I, 190-92). Gautier had seen the pageantry and the pomp; Borrow, typically, had had a grimly realistic meeting with the real man.[14]

In comparison, then, with some other writers of the nineteenth century, Borrow's prose seems at times almost miraculously lucid and vital. As a travel writer, he surpassed most of his contemporaries and richly deserves the compliments they paid his prose. He excelled in three important areas of the travel story: narration, description, and dialogue. We shall take a closer look at each.

II *Narration*

Borrow's *narrative* is chronological rather than causal, except for minor and unhappy exceptions.[15] The method is that of the first person singular. Every page is studded with "I" and "I said." The succession of events is held together only by the fact that all of them represent experiences of the narrator. This is fortunate for Borrow, since he was attracted far more by simple action than by thought. Passages of meditation do not represent him at his best. "It is from action that his imaginative force derives," Augustus Ralli said accurately.[16] This is why *The Bible in Spain* succeeded beyond his other books; it was filled with swift-moving action, free from those bogs of heavy moralizing which mar the pages of *Lavengro* and *The Romany Rye*.

Borrow did not long leave his readers in doubt as to his choice of the chronological method in the Spanish adventure story. The first sentence begins: "On the morning of the 10th of November . . ." The technique continues to the last paragraph of the book, which begins: "Thus had passed Friday, the sacred day of the Moslems. . . ." Plot exists in Borrow's books only if one uses the term as broadly as Rene Wellek when he says, "One of the oldest and most universal plots is that of the Journey, by land or water." [17] Borrow, who travels upon both, makes of his books only what happens in time sequence upon these journeys.

Although the chronological transitions sometimes become rather wooden, the reader is at least saved from dreary accounts of trips and episodes which have no excitement value. Borrow wisely omits his monotonous trips back to England; he treats the Spanish adventure much as if it were one long, unbroken journey. On one occasion, for example, he says simply: "My stay in England was very short, for time was precious, and I was eager to return to the field of action" (*The Bible*, I, 224).

Some of the transitions are not so simply chronological, of course. Not a few of them are strangely abrupt, reminiscent of Sterne. In one place, Borrow has an amusing encounter with a man named Oliban, secretary of the Duke of Rivas, an official who could grant or withhold permission to print the Scriptures in Spain. Discussing matters with Oliban, Borrow finds him forever bringing up the "decrees of the Council of Trent," somewhat fatuously, as if the citation settled everything. When he does it the last time, here is how Borrow makes his transition from that interview to an interview with a different person in a different locale:

All of a sudden, however, he stopped, lifted up his head, seemed to consider a moment, and then, putting his pen behind his ear, he said, "Amongst the decrees of the Council of Trent is one to the effect . . ."

"Oh dear!" said I.

"A singular person is this Oliban," said I to Galiano; "you cannot imagine what trouble he gives me; he is continually talking about the Council of Trent." (*The Bible*, I, 199)

Or Borrow may break off a discussion in the middle, without explanation and without ever returning to it. Once, when his landlord is talking, the conversation ends in this manner:

"Those were merry days, Don Jorge. By the by, I forgot to ask your worship of what opinion you are?"

The next morning whilst I was dressing, the old Genoese entered my room; . . . . (*The Bible*, I, 252)

The unanswered question is left to hang in the reader's memory, tantalizingly; Borrow is playing enigmatic author. But, despite occasional abrupt transitions, Borrow's technique is customarily smooth and chronological.

It is also episodic. Persons appear, are described in terms that suggest they are important, then drop from the story never to be mentioned again. The episodes often take the form of sharply cut vignettes, brief and memorable, free from much of the authorial intrusion which marred so many Victorian adventure stories. Some must rank among the best writing of the century.

The best illustration of this may be the account of Borrow's fight with the Flaming Tinman. Conan Doyle, praising it highly, said that he had seen many great fights himself, often involving the champions of two great countries, but that this account remained for him most vivid of all. "This is the real witchcraft of letters," he said.[18] Sherwood Anderson probably had it in mind when he said of a fight which had been reported to him, "Why, it is as good as George Borrow, beyond which, in praise of writing, no man can go." [19]

Some of Borrow's liveliest writing sets the stage for the great battle. He meets the regal Isopel. Quoting first Norwegian and then gypsy verse to her, he is rewarded by a blow from her hand which almost knocks him down. When the huge Flaming Tinman, a traveling ruffian and kettle mender, appears, Borrow tries to pacify him, but without success. Two quick left jabs from Borrow surprise his surly foe, but do not seriously hurt him. The girl, looking at Borrow doubtfully, says, "You'll never beat the Flaming Tinman in that way." The fight then begins in earnest, with short paragraphs suggesting the breathlessness and fury of it. Borrow does not digress to talk of the nobility of the art of self-defense, the joy of fighting for a young girl's honor, or any of the other philosophical themes which many other Victorian authors might have found implicit in the episode.

Paul Elmer More thought that the "two or three pages in *The Bible in Spain* describing the nocturnal journey from Bembibre to Villafranca . . . for terror and sublimity . . . would be hard to match in any other English book." [20] The best part of the section describes an intense and awesome mountain storm, one lightning bolt of which glared so fiercely that it blinded a mule. The glimpse of a monastery perched on a frightful crag gives Borrow an opportunity to fulminate against Catholicism, but in this place he wisely permits a peasant companion to bring the charges for him. A mountain flood and the passing in the darkness of mysterious and ominous persons complete the terror-filled account.

Only twice does Borrow employ epistolary narrative. A long letter from Isopel Berners plays an important part in the narration involving her, since in it she tells Borrow that there is no hope of their marriage. It is composed in a highly colloquial style and so little differs from Borrow's customary narrative that one would not know it to be a letter without the salutation and farewell (*Romany Rye*, I, 164-67). The other occasion is of almost no significance, being a short epistle from an Armenian of little importance in the story (*Romany Rye*, II, 16).

One other curious technique remains to be mentioned. When gypsies are recounting their life histories, Borrow frequently interrupts them, acting as a kind of interlocutor. A good example is the autobiography of Ursula, the last life story told by any of the gypsies (*Romany Rye*, I, 116-25).

Narrative is Borrow's forte. Wherever one turns in his books there are vividly told stories, long and short. Informal, free from the heavy diction characteristic of so many writers of the time, straightforward in the telling, they remain impressive to the present. They move swiftly; Borrow does not intrude upon them with moralizing reflections. Had he busied himself more with narrative and less with preaching of one kind or another, his later books would probably have succeeded as did *The Bible in Spain*.

III *Description*

Borrow usually employs *description* to accomplish one of three objectives: the fixing of scene or setting as a backdrop for the adventure he narrates; the presentation of guide-book sketches of places, without concern for action, or even, frequently, for relevance to the principal themes of the book; and the characterization of some of the myriads of persons he meets in the course of his travels. In all of these instances he tends generally to preserve the informal manner of his narrative technique.

His fidelity to detail has been warmly praised. Owen McGuire, a Catholic writer with some prejudice against Borrow, commends the accuracy of his description of Petiegua, a village described in *The Bible in Spain* (I, 301-6). McGuire says that Borrow's sketch of the village and of the pastor's house, inside and outside, "is as exact and complete as if they had been photographed for the instruction of a grand jury." [21] The reportorial quality of such descriptions was of great value to Borrow in that it convinced his Victorian readers of his sobriety and truthfulness. And Borrow was even better in his descriptions of natural scenery, where his enthusiasm and photographic powers combined to create superb effects.

He is particularly skillful at picturing nature in her moments of violence and terror. Speaking of the sierras of Spain and Portugal, he describes them as "those singular mountains which rise in naked horridness, like the ribs of some mighty carcass from which the flesh has been torn" (*The Bible*, I, 90). Seeing Finisterra for the first time, he writes of the "granite wall of savage mountains," of the "stern and savage grandeur in everything around," of "flinty and indomitable Spain" (*The Bible*, II, 22-23).

In his portraits of storms on land and sea, Borrow reaches his peak. Almost at once in his tale of the Spanish adventures we are caught up in a storm which has the sea "working like yeast below." Later, an even fiercer tempest tosses Borrow's ship, blowing it hard toward a shore of "steep, abrupt precipices, on which the surf was breaking with the noise of thunder, tossing up clouds of spray and foam to the height of a cathedral." Near nightfall, Cape Finisterra is seen ahead, "a bluff brown granite mountain, whose frowning head may be seen far away by those who traverse the ocean. The stream which poured round its breast was terrific." The mountain, dark and grim, is personified in "head" and "breast," so that an almost human object presents itself to the incredible fury of the elements. The storm's fury mounts:

By about eight o'clock at night the wind had increased to a hurricane, the thunder rolled frightfully, and the only light which we had to guide us on our way was the red forked lightning, which burst at times from the bosom of the big black clouds which lowered over our heads. We were exerting ourselves to the utmost to weather the cape, which we could descry by the lightning on our lee, its brow being frequently brilliantly lighted up by the flashes which quivered around it, when suddenly, with a great crash, the engine broke, and the paddles, on which depended our lives, ceased to play.

The captain is by this time sure that none of the crew "will see the morning." But even though others are ordered below deck, Borrow keeps his station. Vividly, he narrates the violent action taking place until he is ready for some of the finest descriptive writing in the account:

[79]

The lightning enveloped us as with a mantle, the thunders were louder than the roar of a million cannon, the dregs of the ocean seemed to be cast up, and in the midst of all this turmoil, the wind, without the slightest intimation, *veered right about,* and pushed us from the horrible coast faster than it had previously driven us towards it.

(*The Bible,* I, 226-27)

The images are concrete and clear: "mantle, "cannon," "dregs"— all strike a reader as clearly expressive of what Borrow was trying to say in each case. Sound and motion come through vividly in the long triple parallelism, making the storm one of the most vivid in English literature.

Nature's more genial aspects find Borrow not, perhaps, less responsive, but certainly less original in his description. He hears the water rippling over the sand or murmuring softly; the birds sing melodiously; tears of rapture flow (*The Bible,* I, 86-87, 313; *Lavengro,* I, 71). All that can be said for him is that he never over-writes as some of his contemporaries do.[22] But on occasion he effectively throws over a natural scene the gauzy veil of wonder and romance. His description of the view from Elvir Hill is a high moment in *Lavengro* (I, 70-71). Visionary and fairy-like as it is, Borrow makes it minister to his principal interest, man. As he had said himself, "My chief study is man" (*The Bible,* I, 70). And Richard Ford, who knew his attitude well, agreed: "His chief study is man; and therefore, as among the classics, landscape becomes an accessory."[23] So, immediately after setting a highly romantic stage in the Elvir Hill passage, Borrow introduces an abnormally large man who speaks archaic language. The sense of the marvelous is not at all dissipated when the gigantic man fixes precisely the location Borrow has been describing: "Yon river is called the Tweed; and yonder, over the brig, is Scotland" (*Lavengro,* I, 73).

The strangeness with which natural surroundings are presented in the story of the fairy dog and his master (on whose head is a "raw and staring wound" which is never accounted for); in the account of the mysterious blacksmith who, with a word, puts Borrow's great Irish horse into a tempestuous fury, or, with a word, makes him at once calm and gentle; in the tale of the visit to Stonehenge, with all the witchery evoked by the telling—all these are examples of Borrow's occasional departure from the straightforward and realistic description of natural scenes.[24] They are sufficiently infrequent as to make these citations not so much a list of typical examples as a complete catalog.

The pictorial quality of Borrow's sketches has been often commented upon. A Borrow student in 1937 pointed out more fully than anyone had done before the connection between Borrow's excellence in description and his interest in painting.[25] Borrow's brother John was an aspiring artist who had worked under Old Crome and Haydon and in the Louvre. Borrow was also a close friend of Allan Cunningham, author of *Lives of the Most Eminent British Painters* (1829-1833) and of other works on painting. Landscape painting flourished in Norwich, under Old Crome, when Borrow lived there. More importantly, one may find in his own works signs of Borrow's interest in the techniques of painting. He speaks of pictures of the Flood; he praises extravagantly the work of El Greco; he describes a scene in Seville as if he were gazing upon a painting, remarking that "the pencil of Claude himself" would be barely equal to it; and he describes at some length a conversation between his brother and another painter.[26] He believed himself to have been influenced by painting, for he wrote to Murray about the composition of *Lavengro* that the book would consist "of a series of Rembrandt pictures interspersed here and there with a Claude." [27]

In the twenty-sixth chapter of *Lavengro*, Borrow has a description of a sulphurous, stormy day which is unparalleled elsewhere in his writings for pure visual excitement. Too lengthy to reproduce here, it is a riot of unusual cloud shapes, vivid colors (green, orange, black), and striking perspectives (*Lavengro*, I, 282-86). Undoubtedly, his descriptive techniques were influenced by his association with painters and his interest in the art, although it is difficult to make specific assertions of indebtedness. Those who have tried it have agreed neither with one another nor with Borrow.[28]

Borrow's guide-book sketches of localities have been mentioned. They often have no connection with any action or themes; Baedeker-like, they simply point out places of interest for the tourist. This is especially true of *The Bible in Spain, The Zincali,* and *Wild Wales*, of course, where Borrow seems to feel that he is writing, among other things, a travel guide which may be helpful for future visitors.

Often, this kind of set descriptive writing turns out to be well handled and interesting, even for the reader who is anxious to get on with the adventure. For example:

Little can be said with respect to the town of Cordova, which is a mean, dark, gloomy place, full of narrow streets and alleys, without squares or public buildings worthy of attention, save and except its far-famed cathedral; its situation, however, is beautiful and picturesque. Before it runs the Guadalquiver, which, though in this part shallow and full of sand-banks, is still a delightful stream; whilst behind it rise the steep sides of the Sierra Morena, planted up to the top with olive groves. The town or city is surrounded on all sides by lofty Moorish walls, which may measure about three-quarters of a league in circumference; unlike Seville, and most other towns in Spain, it has no suburbs. (*The Bible,* I, 255)

Nothing said here is of any consequence for later action. The talks which Borrow has later in Cordova are not enhanced in any way by this description. The paragraph is simply a concession to the needs of those who, reading the book, may someday resolve to follow in the author's footsteps. His description of the cathedral at Cordova is as good as guide-book writing can be; it has a multitude of details verifiable by visitors and its historical note on the vicissitudes of the structure is informative and entertaining.

Sometimes the guide-book description is more literary than this, however, and Borrow seems carried away by concern for elegance and poetic inversions ("grand are its mountains and no less grand are its plains"); carefully structured parallelisms ("here a deep ravine . . . yonder an eminence . . ." and "little that is blithesome and cheerful, but much that is melancholy"); and rhetorical questions ("And who are the travellers of these districts?"). But, at the other extreme, he becomes too prosaic, writing a guidebook sketch which is inserted into his narrative abruptly and awkwardly, as is his brief and almost grudging concession to the town of Rivadeo: "Rivadeo is one of the principal seaports of Galicia, and is admirably suited for commerce on a deep firth into which the river Mirando debouches. It contains many magnificent buildings, and an extensive square or plaza, which is planted with trees" (*The Bible*, II, 62).

Here Borrow does not even bother to provide himself with a good transitional sentence which will carry his reader smoothly from the narrative into the set-piece of description. He seems to feel that, although Rivadeo must be briefly described for those who will read his book as a tourist's guide, it is unworthy of more than the dryest, most conventional observation. The same thing happens once when, after an exciting meeting between Borrow and the mysterious Swiss treasure-hunter, Benedict Mol, the author descends without any transitional device to the prosiness of "Oviedo contains about fifteen thousand inhabitants. It is picturesquely situated between two mountains . . ." (*The Bible*, II, 84-85).

The foregoing examples have illustrated three different techniques with reference to Borrow's guide-book descriptions. The first showed him at his best, writing informally about a scene in which he obviously had great interest. The second showed him less concerned with the tourist to follow him than with the reader who has an eye for literary style. The third showed him at his prosaic worst, penning little more than map notes. The three include all of Borrow's approaches to that kind of writing.

IV   Characterization and Description

Borrow used another kind of description with great facility. Some of his finest characterizations are done through description. He characterizes little through dialogue, with a few brilliant exceptions. Generally, he expresses his view of personality by lingering upon physical details, using the appearance of the face, clothing, and bodily movements to produce the impression he desires. A good example is his characterization by description of the dwarfish, idiot guide who was to take him to Finisterre:

By this time I had had sufficient time to scan my odd companion from head to foot. His utmost height, had he made the most of himself, might perhaps have amounted to five feet one inch; but he seemed somewhat inclined to stoop. Nature had gifted him with an immense head, and placed it clean upon his shoulders, for amongst the items of his composition it did not appear that a neck had been included.

Arms long and brawny swung at his sides, and the whole of his frame
was as strongly built and powerful as a wrestler's; his body was supported by a pair of short but very nimble legs. His face was very long,
and would have borne some slight resemblance to a human countenance had the nose been more visible, for its place seemed to have
been entirely occupied by a wry mouth and large staring eyes. His
dress consisted of three articles: an old tattered hat of the Portuguese
kind, broad at the crown and narrow at the eaves, something which
appeared to be a shirt, and dirty canvas trousers.   (*The Bible*, II, 6-7)

The guide is so well characterized by this detailed, vivid description that we are not surprised to learn that the fellow, when
talked to, was as like as not to give "a loud laugh, a long leap, and
[clap] his hands thrice above his head." He turns somersaults
frequently—"first-rate somersaults," says Borrow solemnly. His
face "for colour and rigidity might have been of stone." The gro-
tesqueries which the little guide exhibits in the following narrative
are all foreshadowed in the description. One might easily paint his
picture, so minutely is he sketched. Once, inside a small Spanish
hut, the dwarf perceives that Borrow is teasing some strangers by
mimicking their accent. He looks at his master "with a singular
expression, half serious, half droll"; but, saying nothing, he
"slapped his thigh as usual, and with a spring nearly touched the
roof of the cabin with his grotesque head" (*The Bible*, II, 19). It
is a tribute to Borrow's ability to characterize through description
that we should feel, when we read this, that it is precisely what
we should have expected from the guide.

The interest here exhibited in facial features and formation of
the head is found elsewhere in Borrow's characterization through
description. Describing a French criminal in prison with him at
Madrid, he says that the man "had a villainously formed head,
according to all the rules of craniology, and his features were full
of evil expression" (*The Bible*, II, 161). One of his friends once
says to him: "I would you could see his face, Kyrie, it is that of
Judas Iscariot. I think you would say so, for you are a physiogno-
mist" (*The Bible*, II, 290). Borrow himself confesses to his interest in physiognomy when he speaks of a woman in this way: "As I
looked upon her countenance, I said within myself, if there be
truth in physiognomy, thou art good and gentle, O Joanna" (*The
Bible*, II, 384).

[84]

These comments explain Borrow's emphasis upon cranial and facial features as expressive of character. When a strange boy rides a beautiful horse past Borrow, he characterizes him by noting briefly that "there was a disgusting look of sensuality about the mouth" (*The Bible*, II, 397). A new acquaintance has "a long hooked nose, small, twinkling, cunning eyes, and, what I liked worst of all, a continual, sneering smile, which I firmly believe to be the index of a treacherous and malignant heart" (*The Bible*, I, 61). Another stranger has a "face strongly marked and exceedingly expressive; his nose was fine, so was his forehead, and his eyes sparkled like diamonds beneath a pair of bushy brows slightly grizzled." But one thing was wrong: "He had one disagreeable feature—his mouth—which was wide and sensual-looking to a high degree" (*The Bible*, II, 425). These are but a few of the dozens of examples which indicate Borrow's interest in reading character from the expression on the face or from the formation of the head. He especially likes to dwell upon the exceptional or marvelous, the individual tendencies to difference, rather than upon the probable, or ordinary, in human appearance. A gesture habitually repeated, a peculiar walk, a way of looking—any of these may serve to set off a Borrow character.

Sometimes this skill is exhibited in a few bold strokes. A "frightful, ragged object" turns out to be "a girl about eighteen or nineteen, perfectly blind, a white film being spread over her huge, staring eyes" (*The Bible*, II, 234). The mystery of her character is thus suggested; later we learn that she is considered a prophetess by the populace of a small Spanish village. Of an old gypsy woman in Madrid, Borrow says that occasionally she would "stop short, stare in vacancy, and thrust out her palms as if endeavouring to push away some invisible substance; she goggled frightfully with her eyes, and once sank back in convulsions" (*The Bible*, I, 136).

Perhaps such descriptions were possible because Borrow had developed great powers of exact observation and had become, himself, a good mimic. Testifying to that skill, Theodore Watts-Dunton paid Borrow this tribute:

Once, when he was talking to me about the men of Charles Lamb's day—the *London Magazine* set—I asked him what kind of a man was the notorious and infamous Griffiths Wainewright. In a moment Borrow's face had changed: his mouth broke into a Carker-like smile, his eyes became elongated to an expression that was at once fawning and sinister, as he said, 'Wainewright! He used to sit in an armchair close to the fire and smile all the evening like *this*.' He made me see Wainewright and hear his voice as plainly as though I had seen him and heard him in the publisher's parlour.[29]

George Saintsbury added his compliments by saying that he thought Borrow's treatment of coachmen was probably more accurate than Dickens' "rose-coloured representation of Mr. Weller and his brethren." [30] We may conclude that in the short, bold strokes of a moment's vision and in the long, close looks at mannerisms, clothing, countenance, and bodily movement, Borrow is equally adept.

V *Dialogue*

In the purely mechanical sense, Borrow has two ways of indicating *dialogue*. There is, first, the playwriting technique in which the speaker is designated by name and the lines he speaks are separated from his name by a dash. There are no quotation marks. Even when Borrow talks with Antonio, who is to be his intimate companion for a long period, he employs this dramatic technique:

Antonio.—Good evening, brother. . . .
Myself.—Such is my intention. . . .

But within a few paragraphs the conversation of the same pair reverts to the familiar technique:

"I will go with you," I exclaimed. . . .
"Do so, brother," he replied. . . . (*The Bible,* I, 115, 118-19)

There appears to be no reason for Borrow's use of the mechanical contrivance at one time and not at another. In the later books there are still occasional uses of the playwriting technique; but, in proportion to those in the more conventional manner, they are negligible.

The customary technique (lines of direct discourse set off by quotation marks) is used with increasing frequency as Borrow passes from one creative labor to the next. Sometimes he drops the "he said" tags, leaving only the alternate lines of unidentified discourse. The following dialogue has a tempo which sets it apart from that of most Victorian novelists:

"I have read that they were brought by many thousand men."
"Where from?"
"Ireland."
"How did they bring them?"
"I don't know."
"And what did they bring them for?"
"To form a temple, perhaps."
"What is that?"
"A place to worship God in."
"A strange place to worship God in."
"Why?"
"It has no roof."
"Yes, it has."   (*Lavengro*, II, 69-70)

It remains simply unaccountable why Borrow, writing the laconic dialogue above, should revert within another few pages to the visually awkward device of the playwright's page. It is disconcerting to read passages of dialogue with a minimum of directional signs and then to turn abruptly and find the most obvious and distracting markers. The reason is part of the enigma that was Borrow.

Although modern readers enjoy the salty flavor of Borrow's gypsy slang and the provincialisms of the peasants he encounters on his trips, he was criticized for both by contemporaries. Viewed as distractions, the passages were called "mere gibberish to all but gipsies, robbers, and others of their order." [31] Some accused him of aiming after dramatic effect rather than strict verbal accuracy; they felt he should make his meaning clearer by leaving out words requiring a glossary.[32] But the modern reader does not so much mind the effort to be creative, and is concerned principally with whether or not the dialogue is appropriate to the speaker and contributes to the book's aim.

That Borrow's dialogue does often convey a feeling of verisimilitude is clear from the praise which one reviewer gave it. The

Dublin University Magazine refused to apologize for an excessively lengthy extract from *The Bible in Spain*, saying that if other travelers had "the same happy talent for recounting actual conversations, we should have far more lively impressions of the people of distant countries, as well as a more real acquaintance with their modes of life." [33] And at the end of the nineteenth century, George Saintsbury paid homage to Borrow's use of dialogue by saying that he could tell a story in dialogue as well as Defoe and Dumas and that he was their superior in "pure style and in the literary quality of his talk." [34]

Certainly, Borrow makes dramatic improvement as he writes his way through *The Bible in Spain*. The speeches in *The Zincali* had been almost uniformly poor in quality, and generally marked off by the rather obvious theatrical device just discussed. Even in the account of the Spanish tours, Borrow begins slowly. The first chapter, consisting of seventeen pages in the Shorter edition, has only two sentences of dialogue. Both are formal, one being spoken by a sailor and the other by a monk. There is no dialogue at all in the second chapter, and in the third only two brief conversations between Borrow and a man from Palmella.

Even when he finally gets going with longer passages of dialogue, Borrow is inept for a time. When he talks with the three principals of a college in Lisbon, for example, it is impossible to make any distinctions among their speeches, except that the college authorities say "*Blessed* Virgin," whereas Borrow stubbornly insists on saying simply, "Virgin." Otherwise, any one of the speeches could be put into the mouth of any other character without incongruity. All of the speakers are stiffly elegant in speech. Says one: " 'It will afford us extreme satisfaction to show you over it; it is true that satisfaction is considerably diminished by the reflection that it possesses nothing worthy of the attention of a traveler' " (*The Bible*, I, 67-68). Even when allowances are made for the dignity of formal conversation among the Victorians, we find this passage appallingly heavy. It is similarly hard to believe that Borrow actually addressed himself to a drunken mule driver in language so artificial and rhythmic as: "You drunken renegade, who are ashamed to speak the language of your own country, you have broken the staff of your existence, and may now starve" (*The Bible*, I, 55).

The "literary quality" of Borrow's dialogue, which Saintsbury praised, is not always fortunate. In the following example, the contrast between the language of Borrow and the language of his guide is insufficient:

Myself.—Good day to you, my gentleman. The weather is hot, and yonder water appears delicious. I am almost tempted to dismount and regale myself with a slight draught.
Guide.—Your worship can do no better. The day is, as you say, hot; you can do no better than drink a little of this water. I have myself just drunk. . . .   (*The Bible*, II, 13)

Although both speeches are extremely artificial, the reader discovers, as the narrative proceeds, that the guide does not customarily speak like this at all. He and Borrow both speak, generally, in a most informal prose. It is disturbing when, after the colloquial has been established, the reader discovers one or the other lapsing into the most heavily brocaded rhetoric.

Even so, there are isolated instances of skillful dialogue in *The Bible in Spain*, giving promise of better things to come in the later books. Richard Ford was giving good advice during the writing of the Spanish account, and Borrow occasionally listened.[35] In a talk with Galiano, Spanish Minister of Marine Affairs, Borrow conveys through dialogue the quality he has already described in calling Galiano "a very small and irritable man." "Mendizabal is a jackass," Galiano once replies irritably to a query by Borrow. And later, when Borrow says that an effort must be made now in his behalf in the matter of scattering Bibles in Spain, the following response ensued: "'I will do so,' said he, in a waspish tone; for he always spoke waspishly, whether to friend or foe; 'but you must have patience for a few days; we are very much occupied at present'" (*The Bible*, I, 196).

The fullest characterization by dialogue is managed in the case of the guide, Antonio. There are certain "tags" in Antonio's speeches, through several chapters of the narrative; and there is a definite quality of sharp positiveness in what he says. These distinguish him clearly from other characters who appear in the Spanish wanderings. Antonio uses the word "brother" constantly, giving his speech a tribal or religious flavor.[36] He frequently barks

[89]

his sentences explosively: "The swine have killed their brother; would that every Busno was served as yonder hog is. Come in, brother, and we will eat the heart of that hog" (*The Bible*, I, 119-20). Or as in this series of short sentences: "'Good,' said he; 'you may want it. I want none; my passport is the bar lachi. Now for a glass of repani, and then for the road'" (*The Bible*, I, 120). Borrow likes flavoring his dialogue with exotic words from other languages. It is usually gypsy talk, but at times he includes German, French, Latin, Greek, and words from the Scandinavian dialects.[37]

After such lively speech, it is jarring to find passages in which Antonio sounds absurdly pompous. This man, who is said "to be acquainted with all the cut-throats in Galicia" and usually speaks their language, once talks like this:

"I have acquired at various times a great many words amongst the Gallegan domestics in the kitchens where I have officiated as cook, but am quite unable to understand any long conversations. . . . The worst of this language is, that everybody on first hearing it thinks that nothing is more easy than to understand it, as words are continually occurring which he has heard before; but these merely serve to bewilder and puzzle him, causing him to misunderstand everything that is said. . . ." (*The Bible*, I, 372)

This language is obviously that of Borrow, not of Antonio; and the reader wonders about the inconsistency. It is less perplexing when Borrow puts such artificial speech into the mouth of an educated character. When he mentions his old Norwich philosopher friend, William Taylor, for example, he always heightens the style. He has him say such things as: "Oh my respectable and cherished friend, where was it that I had last the felicity of seeing your well-remembered and most remarkable physiognomy?" (*The Bible*, I, 236). The comment appears in the midst of plain prose. Borrow apparently feels that Taylor should always be characterized by the use of involved rhetoric.

Lavengro and *The Romany Rye* represent Borrow's fullest development in skillful use of dialogue. The mercurial exchanges between Borrow and Jasper Petulengro are unusual for the times. Unplagued by mechanical devices, often going for pages at a time without even a single "he said," they are spiced with abrupt answers, gypsy dialect, and the sudden shifts in topic which are characteristic of real conversation.[38]

Borrow's inconsistency in dialogue has been often criticized. Oliver Elton puts very simply the sentiments usually expressed on this score: "The speech of the gipsies, like that of the jockeys and postillions, is sometimes artificially raised and made bookish." [39] But the variance is conveniently explained by John Tilford, a recent Borrow student, who says: "Borrow's 'bookish dialogue' is . . . not speech completely or consistently out of character, but rather that in which there are lapses to a higher level of literacy than one would normally expect from the speaker, lapses which jar the reader because the context is usually appropriate and often racy." [40] Tilford makes the point that Borrow, by refusing to be completely consistent, achieves in his gypsy dialogues an air of wonder and mystery which is artistically more satisfying than absolute realism would have been. He points, by way of example, to the contrast between a speech of Sinfi, in Watts-Dunton's novel *Aylwin,* and one of Jasper Petulengro. At the point of contrast, each character is issuing an invitation. Asking Harry Aylwin to join her tribe, Sinfi says:

You can jine *us* is you like, brother. We're goin' through the West of England with the gries. You're fond o' fishin' and shootin', brother, an' though you're a gorgio, you can't help bein' a gorgio, and you ain't a mumply 'un, as I've said to Jim Burton man's the time; and if you can't give the left-hand body-blow like me, there ain't a many gorgios nor yit a many Romanies as knows better nor you what their fistes wur made for, an' altogether, brother, Beng te tassa mandi if I shouldn't right-on proud to see ye jine our breed. . . .   (Ch. 3, Part viii)

Here is Petulengro's offer to Lavengro:

"You may do that, brother," said Mr. Petulengro, "whether you have money or not. Our tents and horses are on the other side of yonder wooded hill, come and stay with us; we shall all be glad of your company, but more especially myself and my wife Pakomovna."
(*Lavengro,* II, 40)

Borrow omits the heaping up of contractions and thus avoids the wearying effect they have. He avoids also the too-abundant misspellings which Watts-Dunton used to suggest improper pronunciation. By using "wooded hill," "we shall all be glad," and "more especially myself and my wife," Borrow clearly attempts to key the gypsy's talk *above* realism so that Jasper may be remembered as a man of romance and mystery.

Moving back and forth between highly colloquial gypsy talk and highly literary, Borrow achieves some artistic distance between his readers and his characters. His gypsies at times sound real enough to be convincing, but the poetry put into their mouths at other times expresses the sentiments Borrow had about their exotic personalities. He liked creating for them a speech compounded of racy slang, Biblical allusions and rhythm, and here and there a dash of high rhetoric. Watts-Dunton, whose own efforts at gypsy talk are clearly inspired by Borrow, complained that Borrow's gypsies spoke "complex sentences and bookish words which, even among the English people, are rarely heard in conversation." [41] Yet, when Watts-Dunton sought the realism he thought valuable, he lost the romance of the gypsy character; and it is Borrow and not Watts-Dunton who is remembered as the man who wrote about gypsies. There is a higher realism than exact verbal transcription. [42]

But an impression should not be left that all of the inconsistencies in Borrow's dialogue can be so justified. Nothing is more painful than to hear the magnificent Isopel Berners, born in a workhouse and possessed of a vocabulary that reflects the fact, occasionally speaking in the hothouse diction of an aristocratic young gentlewoman. She and Lavengro (Borrow) are outside their tents, once, in Mumper's Dingle as a thunderstorm approaches. Up to this point, she has talked consistently in a bold, direct manner, the language spiced with gypsy words and slang that she has picked up from the Flaming Tinman and his wife. But then Borrow puts these inconceivable words on her lips:

"My dislike is not pretended," said Belle, "I hate the sound of it, but I love my tea and it was kind of you not to wish to cast a cloud over my little pleasures; the thunder came quite time enough to interrupt it without being anticipated—there is another peal—I will clear away, and see that my tent is in a condition to resist the storm, and I think you had better bestir yourself." (*Lavengro*, II, 393)

This comes immediately after some of the best dialogue Borrow ever wrote, the evening talks between himself and Belle over the intricacies of the Armenian verb—with Borrow engrossed in his grammar and Isopel obviously yearning for something more. Perhaps Borrow hoped to change the tone of the scene by giving to Belle such Victorian elegance, but it jars harshly with the dialogue preceding it. There is no good explanation for such inconsistencies.[43]

One other criticism may be brought against Borrow's dialogue. It is occasionally *staged,* losing verisimilitude, despite racy diction, because of its artificial manipulation of material. A talk with Benedict Mol is clearly contrived for Borrow's purposes, with the question-and-answer technique manipulated somewhat clumsily (*The Bible,* I, 206). And a similar Socratic technique is used at great length when Jasper Petulengro and Borrow discuss the definition of a gypsy (*The Romany Rye,* I, 89-90). Fortunately, such staginess in the manipulation of speeches is infrequent.

The general impression from Borrow's books is that he makes steady progress in dialogue skill from the pages of his Spanish adventure story through brilliant conversations in *Lavengro* and *The Romany Rye.* Some of the characterizations he achieves through dialogue are among the finest triumphs in his books. He profited by the conviction Richard Ford once expressed to him: "Dialogues always tell; they are dramatic and give an air of reality."[44]

VI *The Preacher*

It has been suggested already that Borrow's fame among his contemporaries was partially brought about through his expression of a conventional morality and a commonplace philosophy. The non-conformist Evangelical masses who read him through the middle years of the nineteenth century found in his books a faithful expression of their favorite creeds. Borrow knew that occasional preaching was necessary if he were to enjoy popularity. He decided apparently upon a special style for this purpose for it is easy to mark the transition from the generally colloquial style of the travel tales to the elaborate and artificial rhetoric of the moralizing passages. Borrow's musings about ethical and philosophical matters are cloaked in overwrought prose almost as if he were aware of their superficiality.

The lapses into verbiage or evangelical cant, quite unlike his usual forthrightness, were recognized and denounced early. *Tait's Edinburgh Magazine* supposed that most of his sober-minded Christian readers were less disturbed by his wild adventures than by "the incongruous pious ejaculations, the prayers and notices of his preachings, and exhortations with which he has seen meet to interlard the early part of his narrative; as if he felt it the duty of every man engaged in the service of the Bible Society to adopt a certain pious slip-shod phraseology." [45] Whatever the reason, Borrow appears to pull himself up short every now and then, as if recalling that he has a bit of preaching to do on religion, self-reliance, metaphysics, ethics, or the transitoriness of man's stay upon earth and of his glory.

On one occasion, Borrow gives the determined believer's answer to those sceptics who might question the wisdom and providence of God. Speaking of an unnamed friend whose life was miserable until death brought relief, he exonerates the "All-wise" who "did not afflict him without a cause. Who knows but within that unhappy frame lurked vicious seeds which the sunbeams of joy and prosperity might have called into life and vigour? Perhaps the withering blasts of misery nipped that which otherwise might have terminated in fruit noxious and lamentable" (*Lavengro*, I, 25). Theodicy has been more complex than this ever since the writing of Job. All Borrow adds to this commonplace is the heightened style with its parallelisms ("joy and prosperity," "life and vigour," "noxious and lamentable") and the inversion of the final phrase.

How does a man reprove those who annoy or attack him? Borrow works toward a stiff, pompous answer after having had an exciting encounter with a fierce dog. Repelling the animal by staring him "full in the eyes" until he fled, Borrow goes on to say that this device will not work with a "dunghill cur or a terrier, against which a stick or a stone is a much more certain defense." Up to this point, the style is direct and vigorous. But, when Borrow forsakes the narrative to philosophize upon its significance, the style becomes heavily brocaded:

This will astonish no one who considers that the calm reproving glance of reason, which allays the excesses of the mighty and courageous in our own species, has seldom any other effect than to add to the insolence of the feeble and foolish, who become placid as doves upon the infliction of chastisements, which, if attempted to be applied to the former, would only serve to render them more terrible, and, like gunpowder cast upon a flame, cause them, in mad desperation, to scatter destruction around them. (*The Bible*, I, 84)

So many words to say, "Beat the weak, but reason with the strong"! And again there are the parallelisms which Borrow loved so well ("mighty and courageous," "feeble and foolish"). The "who" and "which" clauses clog the passage, modifying phrases slow it painfully near the end.

Not even the heightened style can conceal the shopworn sermonizing of the following comment: "Patience and perseverance generally enable mankind to overcome things which, at first sight, appear impossible. Indeed, what is there above man's exertions? Unwearied determination will enable him to run with the horse, to swim with the fish, and assuredly to compete with the chamois and the goat in agility and sureness of foot" (*Lavengro*, I, 86). Such triteness and heaviness is typical of those for which, as Augustine Birrell once put it, "George Borrow has to be forgiven a great deal." [46]

The reader who has thrilled to Borrow's narrative skill finds it hard to believe his eyes when he encounters the heavy coyness of the following remark: " 'I am afraid,' said I, 'that you are of a turbulent disposition, and that the disputes to which you have alluded are solely to be attributed to the badness of your temper' " (*The Bible*, I, 286). Or: "I deemed it incumbent upon me to be satisfied with a couch in keeping with my manner of journeying, being averse, by any squeamish and over-delicate airs, to generating a suspicion amongst the people with whom I mingled that I was aught higher than my equipage and outward appearance might lead them to believe" (*The Bible*, I, 177). The preachments, threadbare in content, are made ludicrous by the heavy elegance of Borrow's style in the moralizing mood, and they should have been left out.

One of the practices of the day was the extensive use of long, formal apostrophes. Borrow is not guilty of excessive use of them, nor does he compose them in diction any more inflated, pompous, and pretentious than most others one may find in nineteenth-century prose. But they mar his writing. He turns to "thou," "thy," and "thine"; he emphasizes Biblical rhythms and allusions; he cannot bear to let a noun stand unburdened by an adjective. So self-consciously does he enrich the prose that in one sentence the adjective-noun couplets follow upon one another's heels in ludicrously ponderous fashion: "in thy widow's weeds, in the dusky parlour, in the house overgrown with the lustrous ivy of the sister isle, the solitary house at the end of the retired court shaded by lofty poplars" (*Lavengro*, I, 6).

Borrow's apostrophe to his old school may serve as a typical example:

High School!—called so, I scarcely know why; neither lofty in thyself nor by position, being situated in a flat bottom; oblong structure of tawny stone, with many windows fenced with iron netting—with thy long hall below, and thy five chambers above, for the reception of the five classes, into which the eight hundred urchins, who styled thee instructress, were divided. Thy learned rector and his four subordinate dominies. . . . Yes, I remember all about thee. (*Lavengro*, I, 76-77)

The poor pun on the name of the school, the oddly prosaic description of the physical building which is sandwiched in between more elegant sections of the apostrophe—these add nothing to a passage already ruined by "fine writing."

Borrow praised in apostrophes his mother, his favorite river, his country, and his religion; and the effect upon his Victorian readers was good rather than bad. Like Conan Doyle, many of them doubtless viewed most of his apostrophes as "noble pieces of impassioned prose." [47] But, for the modern reader, they are curiously ornate obstructions in the stream of Borrow's narrative prose, and this reader is happiest when safely past one of them.

It remains to be even more specific about Borrow's diction when he sought to impress his readers as moralist or as philosopher. He seldom uses the words which are to follow unless he is deliberately heightening his prose style. One of the most obvious examples is his use of the colorless word "individual" when he means a man or a woman. Augustine Birrell found the word seven times in three pages of *The Romany Rye*.[48] Saintsbury called the habit "a piece of literary gentility of which he, of all others, ought to have been ashamed." [49] Why Borrow, who could write graphically, should have fluctuated so between "the excellent, the adequate, and the regrettable," remains a part of the mystery of his irritating, fascinating personality.[50]

Borrow uses the word "singular" so often that it loses the power to suggest anything unless he follows it by a careful description. Along with "remarkable" and "striking," it is employed often in places where simple description would better fulfill his talent. He uses the word "infinity" to mean an almost unguessable quantity in places where such exaggeration does not fit. He is fond of the word "exhibiting" when he wishes to introduce passages of description, and he likes particularly the phrases "to a degree" and "aspect of nature." All these vague terms are typical of Borrow's writing when he plays the thinker.

The elevated diction characteristic of the reflective passages leads Borrow into rejecting "sneeze" and "swim" in favor of "sternutation" and "natation." He often uses "females" for "women." "Men" are occasionally "bipeds," and "horses" are sometimes "quadrupeds," generally in those sections where Borrow muses rather than narrates. He likes "umbrageous" rather than "shadowy" at times. He decides upon "olfactory organs" when he means "noses" once. "Liquor" is occasionally referred to as "ardent spirits."

The sun may become "the candle of heaven," the eye the "orb of vision," and clear water "the crystal lymph" when Borrow takes it upon himself to elevate his style. He is capable of many "gentle reader" addresses. He can speak of horses and mules who are eating their oats as animals "despatching their provender." He sometimes prefers "ruminating" to "thinking," and "physiognomy" and "lineament" to their more forthright equivalents. Some adjective-noun combinations appear with considerable regularity. Borrow can say "fish" and "birds," but on occasion he speaks of "finny tribe" and "feathered choristers." Gain is often "ill-gotten," views are frequently "noble," and the moon occasionally appears as the "beauteous luminary." The "frugal repast," the "lofty eminence," and the "golden rays" of the sun are equally familiar expressions.

This reluctance to call a spade a spade on one page after it has been bluntly designated on the preceding one is simply a Borrow habit. Pruned of such defects he would be even more pungent, but he would not then present that strange amalgam of techniques which no reader forgets. The stiff, heavy style of the moralizer is clearly discernible wherever one comes upon it in Borrow's prose, and, almost without exception, it descends quickly into triviality and bathos.

VII *The Eccentric in Prose*

It has been pointed out that much of the credit for Borrow's literary successes must be given to the fact that his personality, revealed in his books, captivated thousands who might never have been drawn to him otherwise. Flamboyant, bizarre, unique—all of these adjectives have been applied to that personality. But since Borrow was a writer, it is through the styles he employs that the elements of his personality most fully reveal themselves. We have already seen that his style varies as he works with different motifs in his books; it is equally true that it varies as different aspects of his personality come to the fore. He was humorist, Romanticist, egoist—these and more—and all the facets of his personality clearly shape his style at various times.

Few persons who have read Borrow's books have failed to see that he had a strange, quirky sense of humor. Critics spoke of his "irrepressible love for humor," of "his fund of real racy humor," and of his being a master of the drily comic.[51] Saintsbury, who admired him greatly, spoke of him as "in a certain way, one of the first humorists of our day." [52] The qualification is significant; it indicates that Borrow's technique was not ordinary. Perhaps this explains why some readers have missed seeing anything humorous in Borrow's wry, grave prose. Conan Doyle believed, for example, that in Borrow's works a man would not "from cover to cover, find one trace of any sort of a joke." [53]

Borrow made his own judgment of the quality of his humor. Writing to John Murray about *Lavengro*, he said: "It is full of grave fun and solemn laughter like *The Bible in Spain*." [54] "Grave fun and solemn laughter"—there is perhaps no more accurate description of the essential quality of Borrow's humor. Saintsbury recognized this, too, saying that Borrow belongs to the pre-Addisonian humorists, in a class by himself, and adding that his humor is "rather narrow in range, a little garrulous, busied very often about curiously small matters, but wonderfully observant and true, and possessing a quaint dry savour as individual as that of some wines." [55] The dryness which Saintsbury mentions is achieved in Borrow's prose through restraint, understatement, oddly turned phrases, irony, and some kinds of satire.

This quaint, wry humor was a part of his personality. A. Egmont Hake remembers the serio-comic touches of his talk in this anecdote:

His conversation, too, was unlike that of any other man; whether he told a long story or only commented on some ordinary topic, he was always quaint, always humorous. I was once much amused at hearing him say to my little brother, whom he called the Antelope, "Do you know how to fight a man bigger than yourself? Accept his challenge, and tell him to take off his coat, and while he is doing it, knock him down and then run for your life!" [56]

And a critic for the *English Review*, in 1843, saw Borrow as one of the "most eccentric of mortals" himself, and believed that oddity was the "one essential characteristic of the man and of his book." He felt that pleasure, offense, amusement, and boredom followed one another in succession as one read Borrow's books, but the "one perpetual running commentary must ever be, How very odd!" [57]

Oddities, quaintness—Borrow's books are filled with them, and perhaps most of them come from his habit of exploiting whatever is strange in the personages he meets. Odd himself, he emphasizes the peculiarities which he finds in the characters who people his books. It may be only a touch, as in the portrait of the notary of Pontevedra, or it may be a more extended treatment, like that given to the poet Parkinson, a man who occasionally called at the law office where Borrow spent some five years of apprenticeship as a young man. [58] He can, in spite of the seriousness with which he usually took himself, even laugh at his own person occasionally. Challenged once by the Spanish guard as he came into a city and asked whether he came in the company of a notorious gypsy thief, he asked: "Do I look a person . . . likely to keep company with gypsies?" He pokes quiet fun at himself as he writes: "The national measured me from top to toe, and then looked me full in the face with an expression which seemed to say, 'likely enough'" (*The Bible,* I, 148).

Borrow finds solemn humor in ordinary circumstances simply by falling at once into whatever role fits the occasion. He once met two romantic-looking ecclesiastics at an unnamed village in Spain. They were looking down the road for Don Carlos, pretender to the Spanish throne:

"He may be coming down the road this moment," said I, "for what I know"; and, stepping out, I looked up the way.

The two figures were at my side in an instant. Antonio followed, and we all four looked intently up the road.

"Do you see anything?" said I at last to Antonio.

"Non, mon maitre."

"Do you see anything, sir?" said I to the curate.

"I see nothing," said the curate, stretching out his neck.

"I see nothing," said Pedro, the ex-friar; "I see nothing but the dust which is becoming every moment more blinding."

"I shall go in, then," said I. (*The Bible*, I, 332-33)

And Borrow, who knew all the time that no Pretender was coming through the terrible storm of that night, goes inside, after having made himself briefly a co-worrier with them. His prose is never more lively than at such moments.

Similar humor pervades a bizarre chapter in *Lavengro,* in which Borrow represents his friend, William Taylor, as tracing the philosophical accomplishments of the Germans to their smoking habits. The learned Unitarian and old Norwich friend of Borrow's tells his young visitor that he had best smoke because it keeps men from committing suicide. The talk moves on to the ethics of suicide, with Taylor recalling a gentle female Quaker who decorously caught her blood in a pail so that it would not soil the floor while she was cutting her throat. Gibbon, religion, Christ, Shakespeare, their personal affairs—all are discussed in a serio-comic vein. It is hard to believe that Borrow has not here distorted his original material and shaped it with conscious attention to style for purposes of droll humor. Almost as appealing, although a little more heavy-handed, is the "Taggart took snuff" passage in *Lavengro* (I, 410-11).

Unfortunately, Borrow can overwork sometimes the repetitive

devices. The following effort falls into rather tedious garrulity. Borrow speaks once of an old gentleman, "high respectable," who instructed him in English law: "He has long since sunk to his place in a respectable vault, in the aisle of a very respectable church, whilst an exceedingly respectable marble slab against the neighbouring wall tells on a Sunday some eye wandering from its prayer book that his dust lies below; to secure such respectabilities in death, he passed a most respectable life" (*Lavengro*, I, 269). The gibe at gentility, Borrow's favorite target after Catholicism, would be more effective if the repetition were not so obtrusive. Perhaps it is of such passages that Theodore Watts-Dunton was thinking when he said of Borrow's humor that "while you smile at the pictures it draws, you smile quite as much or more to think that there is a mind so whimsical, crotchety, and odd as to draw them." [59]

Borrow is occasionally the gentle satirist. Speaking once of a certain majestic lie, he says: "But when did a calumnious report ever fall to the ground in Spain by the weight of its own absurdity?" (*The Bible*, I, 292-93). He attributes to a dapper little man in attendance upon Lord Byron's funeral these unconsciously pompous words: "Great poet, sir . . . but unhappy, a fate of genius, sir; I, too, am frequently unhappy" (*Lavengro*, I, 385). He has great fun satirizing pedantry, as in the case of the poetaster Parkinson (*Lavengro*, I, 202-7). He can, at times, even be mildly satirical—and therefore humorous—about Catholicism; but in most places the attack passes beyond satire to a slashing invective so deadly and malicious that one only winces.

Borrow is never ludicrously comical; he never unbends that far. Unlike his contemporary Dickens, he is unable or unwilling to mix humor with pathos. Nor does he approach the genius of Thackeray that could conceal beneath a light exterior a depth of meaning and a world of thought which Borrow could not fathom. He is not playful, although once or twice he seems to try playfulness, but it comes off clumsily. Perhaps he is more like Bulwer-Lytton and Kingsley in that, like them, he makes his humor subservient to a higher purpose. His humor is generally that of the Christian gentleman who permits himself a wry smile at the absurdities of society as he presses on in his various callings—colporteur, linguist, enlightened wanderer.

. . .

Sometimes Borrow's personality expresses itself through Romantic prose, touching the scenes and events around him with an airy, gossamer quality. He uses archaic diction, rich allusiveness, and his interest in ancient languages and history to contrast with his usual plain style. He turns from the hard-headed and practical realist—who could fear God but knew how to take his own part, who knew how to use a strong right arm and to outwit the most cunning bandits—to the dreamer with a predilection for the mysterious, the remote, the strange, and the fantastic. It is probably the romance of exotic and half-forgotten languages which drew Borrow to them in the first place, since he never seems deeply concerned about scientific accuracy.

The whole Spanish adventure has been viewed as a Romantic adventure, with Borrow playing a role similar to Don Quixote's in its whimsy and in its futility. Shane Leslie, writing in the *Dublin Review,* said of Borrow: "He has been called 'a fantastic bigot,' but he is better dubbed a 'Biblical Don Quixote'—one, indeed, who, for the entertainment of Catholic and Protestant alike, carried out a campaign against a visionary Giant Pope, as fond and futile as the famous cavalry charge, executed by one nobler and madder than he, among the unheeding windmills of La Mancha." [60] The idea is an attractive one, especially when one remembers that Borrow really accomplished almost nothing in Spain so far as proselyting was concerned. Yet so romantic an affair did he make it at times that one is likely to forget his failures and to view the entire campaign as a gloriously successful battle between one brave man and the hosts of the enemy.

Perhaps the most perceptive comments ever made about Borrow's abilities as a Romantic writer were written by Arthur Conan Doyle. Doyle had read Borrow's account of the skulls of the long-dead Danes, an archaic and poetic account of a collection in the little village church in Hythe. In this passage, Borrow is highly evocative, throwing the air of mystery and romance over the scene he describes. He uses phrases like "Spirit of eld, what a skull was yon!" and "ancient chronicles of the north." He tantalizes his reader with mention of secrets which would astonish and awe him if he could but learn them. And he says that this one encounter forever after shaped his concepts of the entire Danish race and language. It is a pleasant coincidence that Doyle also saw these skulls and recorded his impression of them. He found them "rather below the human average," and concludes that Borrow romanticized them. His comment on the stylistic techniques used to do this is excellent:

But he [Borrow] had one great and rare gift. He preserved through all his days a sense of the great wonder and mystery of life—the child sense which is so quickly dulled. Not only did he retain it himself, but he was word-master enough to make other people hark back to it also. As he writes you cannot help seeing through his eyes, and nothing which his eyes saw or his ear heard was ever dull or commonplace. It was all strange, mystic, with some deeper meaning always struggling to the light. If he chronicled his conversation with a washer-woman, there was something arresting in the word he said, something singular in her reply. If he met a man in a public house, one felt, after reading his account, that one would wish to know more of that man. If he approached a town he saw and made you see—not a collection of commonplace houses or frowsy streets, but something very strange and wonderful, the winding river, the noble bridge, the old castle, the shadows of the dead. Every human being, every object, was not so much a thing in itself as a symbol and reminder of the past. He looked through a man at that which the man represented. Was his name Welsh? Then in an instant the individual is forgotten and he is off, dragging you in his train, to ancient Britons, intrusive Saxons, unheard-of bards, Owen Glendower, mountain raiders and a thousand fascinating things.[61]

The last four sentences admirably suggest one of the ways Borrow has of touching the prosaic with wonder. Characters he meets often become symbols of a lost and unremembered art, a forgotten race, a neglected tongue. Doyle's references to the washerwoman, the man in a tavern, the approach to a town, the man of Welsh background are all specific; each incident appears in Borrow's books.

It is sometimes his technique to suggest the romantic by avoiding the explicit mention of proper names. He describes Old Sarum in *Lavengro* and also fully describes Salisbury, but he never once names either of them (II, 71, 74-76). In the masterful fifth chapter of *Lavengro*, we are introduced to the gypsies, although there is not a word written as to what people they actually are. In the next chapter Borrow says, "Years passed on, even three years," and there is still no word about the identity of these people who had so obviously caught his fancy. Many chapters later he meets Jasper, one of the gypsies, for the second time. This time he almost names the people, but again stops short. "You are one of them," said I, "whom people call ———" (*Lavengro*, I, 168). His references to Norwich and to Oulton, his earlier and later homes, are made similarly. He hints, insinuates, drops vague clues as to his precise meaning, but no more. This manner once caused a writer for the *People's Journal* to complain that in Borrow's books "curiosity must be excited . . . not to be gratified, but to be tantalized within an inch of its life till it dies of sheer exhaustion." [62]

This cloudiness with respect to places and persons is also occasionally thrown over times. The account of Byron's funeral is touched with a strange magic. As he stands watching the hearse pass, talking meanwhile with "a dapper-looking individual," Borrow seems hardly to know who Byron is. He meditates upon poets, wonders whether Byron was *really* unhappy or only posing, marvels that the sun flames out upon the procession as if doing honor to the dead poet, and concludes that " 'Childe Harold' and that ode" will cause the dead man to be remembered. The separate elements of this account seem prosaic enough, but the total narrative has a quality of remoteness and unreality (*Lavengro*, I, 381-83).

The "king of the vipers" episode in *Lavengro* (I, 44-47) is a good example of Borrow's abilities in this mood. Too lengthy for reprinting here, the passage has the flavor of mystery but achieves verisimilitude by the narrator's insistence upon concrete details. The old man who tells the story repeats several times what his exact position on the ground was when he encountered the king of the vipers. The fact that he cannot remember whether the ground had been planted in oats or in barley before the harvest is a technique of uncertainty about *irrelevant* details which Defoe used long before in such a tale as "The Apparition of Mrs. Veal." There is nothing really improbable in the narrative, nothing supernatural at least; and yet a gauze of romance and unreality hangs between it and the reader's eye.

The *locus classicus* for illustrating Borrow's romantic nature is the famed "wind on the heath" passage from *Lavengro* (I, 273-

75). Few books or essays ever printed about Borrow have omitted this passage.[63] It is prepared for when Borrow, wandering along the heath, "came to a place where, beside a thick furze, sat a man, his eyes fixed intently on the red ball of the setting sun." The man was Borrow's friend Jasper, who told Borrow that since they last met his father and mother had died. Borrow then asks the gypsy for his opinion of death:

"When a man dies, he is cast into the earth, and his wife and child sorrow over him. If he has neither wife nor child, then his father and mother, I suppose; and if he is quite alone in the world, why, then, he is cast into the earth, and there is an end of the matter."
"And do you think that is the end of a man?"
"There's an end of him, brother, more's the pity."
"Why do you say so?"
"Life is sweet, brother."
"Do you think so?"
"Think so! There's night and day, brother, both sweet things; sun, moon, and stars, brother, all sweet things; there's likewise the wind on the heath. Life is very sweet, brother; who would wish to die?"
"I would wish to die—"
"You talk like a gorgio—which is the same as talking like a fool— were you a Romany chal you would talk wiser. Wish to die, indeed! A Romany chal would wish to live forever!"
"In sickness, Jasper?"
"There's the sun and stars, brother."
"In blindness, Jasper?"
"There's the wind on the heath, brother; if I could only feel that, I would gladly live forever."

Only the middle part of this, beginning "Life is sweet" and ending, "who would wish to die?" is usually anthologized. But a more accurate picture of Borrow's approach to and departure from this high moment of Romantic style is given by making the extract larger. The somber acceptance of human fate in the first few lines gives added power to the unquenchable and perhaps illogical *joie de vivre* which Jasper expresses. Sick or blind, one may still experience the great elemental forces of nature; the wind on the heath blows cleanly; life is sweet and zestful. This is not Romanticism of the moonlight school, where fairies, goblins, and witches enchant. It is a sunlight variety, where bodies participate energetically in any dreams of the mind. It is a "racing" Romanticism, not a counterpane variety. This strangely quick responsiveness to the bizarre and the fabulous in his environment is another aspect of Borrow's many-sided personality, and he employs for it a special prose style quite different from his usual plainness.

CHAPTER 4

The Biblical Touch

MANY critics of Borrow's style have observed that he was indebted to the Bible. F. W. Robberds, writing a review in 1851, was outraged by Borrow's "Hebraisms." [1] A recent survey of the English novel includes the comment that Borrow's style "is a mixture of Biblical idiom, roguish jargon, and simple straightforward writing." [2] But no one has given more than passing notice to this element in Borrow's prose—nor has anyone examined the matters of quantity, purpose, and consistency in the employment of Biblical rhythms and allusions. The influence of the Bible upon Borrow's writing is actually so pervasive and, in some cases, so strangely expressed, as to call for separate treatment.

The most striking fact about Borrow's employment of Biblical touches is that he is completely unpredictable and inconsistent. He appears to "turn on" the Biblical style at times with full consciousness of what he is doing, but at others he falls into the mannerism without any discoverable purpose. If the Biblical idioms had been simply an integral part of his literary manner, so that they welled up without conscious thought while he composed, there would be a degree of consistency about his prose. But if the style were deliberately appropriated at certain moments for some special purpose, it would not be surprising to find abrupt entrances into the style and equally abrupt departures from it.

This practice is precisely what a reader does find. Borrow suddenly begins to write in a heavily Biblical style, remains consistent in it for a few paragraphs or even a few pages, and then as abruptly forsakes it for a markedly different prose. If it could be demonstrated that he always used the Biblical style for certain persons, or in restricted circumstances, a reader might believe that he was at least careful about what he was doing. But the fact is that he is inconsistent even when the same characters continue to speak and act in the same setting. They may begin speaking the Biblical idioms and end the scene in prose bearing no resemblance to them at all. Part of this is sheer carelessness; part of it depends on that self-conscious dramatizing which was so essential an ingredient in Borrow's personality. It pleased him to think of himself as another Paul, sent out to evangelize the heathen. He stresses constantly the special qualifications of language, physical prowess, cunning, and spiritual maturity which qualified him for the task. Undoubtedly, he occasionally appropriates the Biblical style to remind readers of the nature of his mission, something which might otherwise be forgotten in the sweep and movement of pure adventure. Once stamped as Christian *picaro* after his Spanish account appeared, Borrow simply kept on playing the role at times in the composition of the Romantic autobiographies.

It should be said at this point that much of Borrow's prose has a swing to it which is not necessarily the result of his Bible reading. The four "ands" in the following extract produce the rhythmical swing of "natural" narrative, of child's talk: "I heard the village clock strike the hours until midnight, and from midnight till four in the morning, when I sprang up and began to dress, and despatched my servant to hasten the man with the mules, for I was heartily tired of the place and wanted to leave it" (*The Bible*, I, 21). And one has only to read aloud the following selection to prove how unmistakably established the rhythms can be in some of Borrow's long sentences: "When many years had rolled on, long after I had attained manhood, and had seen and suffered much, and when our first interview had long since been effaced from the mind of the man of peace, I visited him in his venerable hall, and partook of the hospitality of his hearth" (*Lavengro*, I, 161).

The longest unbroken section of that sentence ends with the markedly rhythmic "from the mind of the man of peace," where two anapests and an iamb, united with alliteration, set up the most obvious pattern in the selection. This comes close to a formula associated also with much of the poetic prose of the Bible, especially as illustrated in Job, Ecclesiastes, and parts of the prophetic books. A sentence chosen by Saintsbury as typically Biblical is found, upon analysis, to contain six anapestic feet.[3] But it takes something more than similarity in rhythm to approximate Biblical style, as shall be pointed out later.

The examples above are meant to show that there is much prose in Borrow's works which is rhythmical, although not necessarily indebted to the Bible. Such rhythmical prose probably arose from Borrow's knowledge of the reading habits of mid-nineteenth century audiences. "It must be remembered," says a student of Victorian reading techniques, "that, in this early nineteenth century, reading aloud was far more common than it is now." [4] Borrow has only to heighten the natural iambic roll of English prose in order to get some of the memorable rhythms which, as one Borrovian put it, "pursue the reader as the long-drawn ebb of the sea pursues the traveler who turns his steps inland." [5]

But having made this distinction, it is possible to turn to those passages in which Borrow obviously appropriates a Biblical manner. There is, of course, no single "Biblical style," but for purposes of convenience this chapter assumes one. Rhythm alone is not sufficient evidence of Biblical influence, even when the rhythm can be precisely matched with a passage from the Bible. Both diction and allusion play an important part, along with imagery, and perhaps a couple of these must be present in combination with the rhythm before one can say with assurance that he has found a Biblical touch.

C. S. Lewis argues that to isolate rhythm from imagery and diction is to falsify the approach to a study of Biblical style. He believes that, taken alone, the "influence of the rhythms of the Authorized Version are very hard to detect." Since these Biblical rhythms "are in fact extremely various, and some of them are unavoidable in the English language," he doubts that a rhythm, unless there is some other resemblance or association present, is recognizable as Biblical. He presents this example: "At the regatta Madge avoided the river and the crowd," and asks whether this would, without any warning, remind a reader of: "At the beginning God created the heaven and the earth." [6]

What must be looked for, then, is a combination of rhythm, diction, imagery, and allusion. This strongly suggests that Borrow has at that point decided to appropriate the Biblical style. And there are many places where even the most superficial reading can hardly leave one in doubt. Borrow repeatedly begins sentences or paragraphs with the formula: "And it came to pass." [7] He is fond of "thou," "thine," "ye," "oft," and similar words commonly associated with the King James version of the Bible. It may also be true that he uses a kind of elevated diction which derives from his having much read the Bible, but this characteristic would be harder to trace. It is what Lewis means when he says that he suspects, without proof positive, that it is due to the influence of the Bible that English writers, at elevated moments,

tend to speak of corn and wine rather than of beef and beer and butter, of chariots rather than chargers, of rain rather than sunshine as a characteristic blessing, of sheep more often than cows and of the sword more often than either the pike or the gun, if bread rather than mutton or potatoes is their lofty synonym for food, if stone is more poetical than brick, trumpets than bugles and fine linen loftier than satin and velvet.[8]

The best way of illustrating Borrow's appropriation of Biblical style, as well as his inconsistency in the matter, is to extract generously from his books. Beginning with a mild example, we find Borrow in prison at Madrid, gazing upon a fellow prisoner who is musing. Borrow reflects:

His mind was perhaps wandering in that dreadful valley of the shadow, into which the children of earth, whilst living, occasionally find their way: that dreadful region where there is no water, where hope dwelleth not, where nothing lives but the undying worm. This valley is the facsimile of hell, and he who has entered it has experienced here on earth for a time what the spirits of the condemned are doomed to suffer through ages without end. (*The Bible*, II, 165)

The phrases, "valley of the shadow," "hope dwelleth not," and "the undying worm," are obvious Biblical reminiscences. The style is not inappropriate in this particular place, perhaps, but a man with surer sensitivity for words might not have used the prosaic "facsimile" in the midst of this poetic philosophizing.

Sometimes Borrow tries only to impart a more romantic touch to his narrative. He may begin a completely prosaic account of his schooling by saying, "Years passed on, even three years," and then never return in the rest of the chapter to a Biblical manner, except for the scattered "And it came to pass" formulas (*Lavengro*, I, 63). He may open a chapter with these straightforward words: "I was standing on the castle hill in the midst of a fair of horses," and continue in the plainest of prose to describe the castle and its surroundings. Then suddenly he repeats the first paragraph, only this time with Biblical flavor: "So it came to pass that I stood upon this hill, observing a fair of horses" (*Lavengro*, I, 162). There is nothing else Biblical in the chapter.

Borrow can insert, inexplicably, a Hebraism into the prosiest description: "Little can be said with respect to the town of Cordova, which is a mean, dark, gloomy place, full of narrow streets and alleys, without squares or public buildings worthy of attention, save and except its far-famed cathedral" (*The Bible*, I, 255). The Biblical parallelism contrasts starkly with the plain prose of the rest of this passage. Once, after a long description of the lackadaisical reactions of certain Moors in places that should have stirred them with pride, Borrow departs abruptly from his plain style and says: "Yet these men were hajis and talebs, men likewise of much gold and silver—men who had read, who had traveled, who had seen Mecca and the great city of Negroland" (*The Bible*, I, 257). The phrase, "men likewise of much gold and silver," shouts out its Biblical origins in this passage.

There is some evidence that Borrow is led into more pronounced use of Biblical rhythm and diction when he is talking with, or about, a clergyman. He is impressed once by a Methodist minister whom he encounters upon a heath, preaching to a crowd of laboring people. He quotes at length from the preacher's sermon, but, oddly enough, the style of the sermon itself is not noticeably Biblical. However, Borrow's own reminiscences suddenly begin to partake of the Biblical manner. "I saw thee once again," he says of the preacher, whose black locks "were become grey, even like my own." And as he listens, a man dashes by on horseback, whispering excitedly, "Why loiterest thou here?—knowest thou not all that is to be done before midnight?" Borrow departs, waving to the preacher and saying, "the seed came up at last, after a long period!" After this allusion to the parable of the sowers, he concludes: "Would that my life had been like his—even like that man's!" (*Lavengro*, I, 272-73).

Other passages support the idea that Borrow appropriates the Biblical manner more emphatically when a clergyman is involved, but he is so inconsistent that it is not possible to say that this

explains his use of Biblical rhythms on these occasions. For example, he is once writing without any hint of the Biblical in his style
when he suddenly opens a paragraph with: "And it came to pass
that, as we were seated over the Cyprus wine, we heard a
knock . . ." (*Lavengro*, II, 7). Since a rabbi enters, one might
suppose he had discovered the reason for the Biblical formula, but
it is quickly dropped and not used again.

Even when Borrow becomes a preacher himself, he is inconsistent in his use of the manner. Near the end of his account of the
Spanish trips, he reminds one of the soaring rhetoric of the great
Hebrew prophets as he speaks the apostrophe to England's glory.
Assuming the prophet's wisdom and predictive ability, Borrow
tells England what to do in highly Biblical styles, promising her a
great future under God if she will listen:

Arouse thee, whilst yet there is time, and prepare thee for the combat
of life and death! Cast from thee the foul scurf which now encrusts
thy robust limbs, which deadens their force, and makes them heavy
and powerless! Cast from thee thy false philosophers. . . . And re-
move from thee the false prophets who have seen vanity and divined
lies; who have daubed thy wall with untempered mortar, that it may
fall; who see visions of peace where there is no peace; who have
strengthened the hands of the wicked, and made the heart of the righteous sad.   (*The Bible*, II, 327-29)

Yet even within this passionate sermon, Borrow can write a sentence as involved and cumbersome as this: "Becoming, ere ex-
tinct, a scorn and a mockery for those selfsame foes who now,
though they envy and abhor thee, still fear thee, nay, even against
their will, honour and respect thee!" (*Lavengro*, I, 239-40). One is
hard put to know why Borrow should switch from so intensely
Biblical a manner to rhetoric as artificial and pompous as any contemporary bombast.

At the house of an Antinomian preacher, Borrow asks for a
Bible in Danish. The preacher says: "Truly, I have it not; but, as
you are a customer of mine, I will endeavour to procure you one,
and I will write to that laudable society which men call the Bible
Society, an unworthy member of which I am, and I hope by next
week to procure what you desire" (*Lavengro*, I, 239-40). This
passage is rather awkwardly Biblical at one moment but not so at

the next. Borrow's reply is momentarily consistent with the mannerism: "And when I heard these words of the old man, I was very glad, and my heart yearned towards him; and I would fain enter into conversation with him, and I said. . . ." Here, however, although the conversation continues, all vestige of Biblical rhythm, diction, and imagery ceases abruptly.

Frequently, Borrow has his Jewish characters employ the Biblical rhythms, although they are just as likely to drop it altogether a moment later. A Gibraltar Jew, early in the Spanish story, suddenly swings, at the end of his speech, into the rhythm and diction of the Bible: "Pay her therefore the price, that we may then forthwith sell the mantle and divide the gain" (*The Bible,* I, 75). The speaker, Judah Lib, is made to speak Biblically at one moment, quite plainly the next. Sometimes Borrow even switches Lib's speech patterns *within sentences* during the eight-page passage.

Another Jew, who meets Borrow as he is about to enter the Spanish town of Ocana, issues a warning couched in only faintly Biblical language. But in the final sentence he becomes strongly Biblical: "Fear nothing for your servant, for he is known to the alcade, and will be set at liberty; but do you flee, and may God attend you" (*The Bible,* II, 222). An old moor whom Borrow meets near the end of his stay in Spain is also made to talk Biblically at times, quite prosaically at others, until at last Borrow has him speak like this:

Good are our horses, and good our riders, yea, very good are the Moslems at mounting the horse; who are like them? I once saw a Frank rider compete with a Moslem on this beach, and at first the Frank rider had it all his own way, and he passed the Moslem, but the course was long, very long, and the horse of the Frank rider, which was a Frank also, panted; but the horse of the Moslem panted not, for he was a Moslem also. . . . (*The Bible,* II, 399)

The first two clauses of the second sentence stand in the midst of this deliberately Biblical passage with as much propriety as a Gentile in the Holy Place of the Temple, but Borrow does it often and inexplicably.

It is hard to believe that an old priest spoke as Borrow represents him:

Should these dark days pass by, Don Jorge, and you should be in these parts, I hope you will look in upon me, and I will show you my little library of the fathers, and likewise my dovecote, where I rear numerous broods of pigeons, which are also a source of much solace, and at the same time of profit. (*The Bible*, I, 262)

Even less believable is the comment, cast in the language of Luke 11:7, which Borrow represents a gruff voice as making when shelter is requested: "Trouble me not: the door is now shut, and my children are with me in bed; I cannot arise to let you in" (*The Bible*, I, 359). Nor can one believe that the strange character called Antonio de la Trava really spiced his language here and there with such constructions as: "Think not that I would toil along these sands with you. . . ." (*The Bible*, II, 37).

In addition to the many places where Borrow employs Biblical rhythms in combination with Biblical imagery and diction, there are perhaps several hundred scattered allusions in his books to Biblical subject matter. These usually stand alone, that is to say, without Biblical rhythms; and sometimes they are sufficiently absorbed into the text as to be difficult to identify. Some are direct and obvious; some, quite obscure. An entire narrative may be colored by the technique of frequent allusion to the Bible, although without recourse to Biblical rhythm, imagery, or diction.

The account of the storm at sea off Cape Finisterre is an example. Borrow appears to be influenced by the account of Paul's shipwreck on Malta. Like Paul, Borrow is the only calm man on board. He stands his station "though almost drowned with water"; and, as with Paul, there comes at last the miraculous delivery. The influence is perhaps pointed up by the statement that "the oldest sailors on board acknowledged that they had never witnessed so providential an escape." Borrow responds: "I said from the bottom of my heart, 'Our Father, hallowed be Thy name.'" (*The Bible*, I, 225-28).

On another occasion, when Borrow is asked to leave the Madrid prison into which he was thrown by error, he simply quotes Acts 16:37 without identifying the verse and lets that stand as his answer (*The Bible*, II, 154). Thinking of his mission to spread the Gospel of the written word in Madrid, he echoes Paul's response to the Macedonian call: "I had, however, no fears, and had full confidence that the Lord would open the path before me to Madrid" (*The Bible*, I, 229; cf. Acts 16:6-11). He apologizes for comparing himself with Paul at Ephesus, but he says that, like Paul, he was "fighting with wild beasts" (*The Bible*, II, 118; cf. I Cor. 15:32). He heads a chapter with the comment: "It is hard to kick against the pricks," another allusion to Paul, and calls it a proverb, which it may or may not have been (*Lavengro*, I, 345; cf. Acts 9:5).

Other New Testament allusions show his familiarity, not only with Paul's life and epistles, but with the gospels and with letters written by other apostles. "When threatened by danger," he says, "the best policy is to fix your eye steadily upon it, and it will in general vanish like the morning mist before the sun" (*The Bible*, I, 39-40; cf. James 4:14). Trying to get an old shopkeeper to sell Bibles to his apathetic countrymen, Borrow says to him that "if he were anxious to help lay the axe to the root of superstition and tyranny," he might do so by peddling these books (*The Bible*, I, 36; cf. Matt. 3:10). A native of St. James of Compostella, talking of the superiority of his town over nearby Coruna, says: "But what good can come from Coruna?" (*The Bible*, I, 408; cf. John 1:46). He speaks of the great fighter, Belcher, "who is gone to his place" (*Lavengro*, I, 279; cf. Acts 1:25).

Speaking to Count Ofalia, he says: "I replied that, like the Pharisees of old, they cared more for the gold of the temple than the temple itself" (*The Bible*, II, 135; cf. Matt. 23:16-17). Only the reference to the Pharisees keeps this from being an obscure allusion, even for Bible readers. Finally, the words of a Jew about Mrs. Borrow's unborn son were reported to her, and she "treasured them in her heart" (*Lavengro*, I, 13; cf. Luke 2:19). These are examples of many such allusions to the New Testament.

Borrow is equally familiar with the Old Testament. He speaks of "the manna which dropped from heaven," of "the spring which suddenly gushed from the flinty rock" (*The Bible*, II, 218; cf. Exodus 16-17). Speaking of his Bible distribution, he says: "Many a book which is abandoned to the waters is wafted to some remote shore, and there proves a blessing and a comfort to millions, who are ignorant from whence it comes" (*The Bible*, I, 40; cf. Eccles. 11:1). He paraphrases Job 5:1 when he says, "For, as the sparks fly upward, so is man born to trouble" (*Lavengro*, I, 184). Speaking of the three college principals at Lisbon, he says: "I had stumbled upon their shibboleth, and proclaimed myself an Ephraimite, and not of Gilead" (*The Bible*, I, 69; cf. Judges 12:5-6). And speaking to the departed spirits of the rector and church clerk in his home church, he says: "By this time ye are probably gone to your long homes" (*Lavengro*, I, 34; cf. Eccles. 12:5).

These typical allusions make it obvious that Borrow had ready at hand a comprehensive knowledge of Biblical incidents and Biblical prose styles, a fact not surprising in view of his own testimony about his childhood:

Twice every Sunday I was regularly taken to the church, where, from a corner of the large spacious pew, lined with black leather, I would fix my eyes on the dignified high-church rector, and the dignified high-church clerk, and watch the movements of their lips, from which, as they read their respective portions of the venerable liturgy, would roll many a portentous word descriptive of the wondrous works of the Most High. (*Lavengro*, I, 33-34)

His mother, defending him against the anger of his father, says that "he is not a bad child, after all," and that "he is always ready to read the Bible." This pacifies Mr. Borrow, who loved to hear the Bible read to him, and who must often have said, "he shall read the Bible to us this night" (*Lavengro*, I, 221). One wonders how many week nights, following those two-a-Sunday services, young Borrow sat in the house reading the words of Scripture aloud to his parents. At one period, Borrow says that he was devoting most of his time to his father. "I read the Bible to him, which was his chief delight" (*Lavengro*, I, 296).

A. Egmont Hake, writing in 1881, said of Borrow that "he read very little, and had few books except old ones in foreign tongues, and a Hebrew Bible which he studied through life." [9] From chilhood to old age, then, Borrow had ever at hand the rhythms, parallelisms, imagery, and diction of the Bible. His natural interest in Biblical prose may also have been accentuated by his publisher, Murray. Hake, telling some anecdotes about Murray, says the publisher would "double his fist and exclaim, 'I want to meet with good writers, but there are none to be had; I want a man who can write like Ecclesiastes!'" [10]

The Biblical Touch

It would seem, in view of the foregoing, that Borrow used Biblical rhythms, diction, and imagery on certain occasions when he felt they would suggest his missionary work and also, perhaps, increase the sense of mystery and romance. He uses the Biblical mannerisms capriciously, sometimes with telling effect—adding the flavor of the antique, the remote, and the bizarre to his narrative—sometimes with much awkwardness and inconsistency, sliding in and out of the Biblical manner in a way that borders upon the ludicrous. There is no hint that he himself saw how haphazardly he had employed this thing which was so much a part of him from childhood. But that it pervades his style and is responsible for some of the best and some of the worst of him, there is no doubt.

CHAPTER 5

The Disciple

IT HAS been common to speak of Borrow's lack of technical equipment for writing and to say that he learned little from others.[1] In the year of Borrow's greatest success, a reviewer styled him "sui generis" and said he stood "apart and aloof from all his literary compeers." [2] The author of a study of vagabonds in literature says that the comparisons made between Borrow and others, whatever affinities are discovered, only serve ultimately to point up the former's originality.[3] One of Borrow's closest friends and most ardent champions believed that "there was scarcely a point in which he resembled any other writer of his time." [4]

There can be no question of Borrow's standing *aloof* from his literary colleagues, even from the one or two whose works he appreciated. A partial cause was his eccentricity as a reader. He admitted in *Lavengro* that during several years in London he never read a newspaper of any description. He felt much the same about contemporary literary discussions, either refusing to enter into them except upon his own narrow grounds, or delivering so abrupt and tactless a dictum that the talk died. He makes no references to Tennyson, Thackeray, Macaulay, Dickens, or Carlyle in his works, although they were comtemporaries whose names were on the lips of readers and publishers. It is quite possible that he simply knew very little about them from firsthand reading, with Dickens a modified exception. His reading, though deep in some obscure areas, was narrow. Theodore Watts-Dunton tells a humorous story of Borrow's knowledge of one Ambrose Gwinett, whose adventures had been narrated in a "very scarce eighteenth century pamphlet." [5] Borrow certainly knew some obscure literature of the eighteenth and nineteenth centuries, especially when it dealt with eccentric persons and exotic languages. He knew the works of many Scandinavian poets, some so minor as to be un-

known even to well-read contemporaries. But there is no evidence
that he labored to understand the major literary figures of his
time.

It is likely that something more than eccentric reading habits is
responsible. Borrow liked to stand apart from other men; he cultivated the pose. In his more or less solitary journeys, he indulged
the craving; he was, as one of his biographers later put it, "lord of
the open road." It may have been a part of his act to turn deliberately away from men who were widely discussed in literary circles
to obscure writers upon whom only he could make authoritative
comments. Whatever the reasons—although Dickens, Tennyson,
and Browning were household names in his prime—Borrow over-
looks them to talk extravagantly of forgotten Danes and unknown
Welshmen.

His dislike of the whole world of literary reputations and publishers may also have played a part. From the time of his early
mishaps with Sir Richard Phillips to the later quarrels with John
Murray, he got along poorly with them. His fierce egotism lent
itself poorly to editorial curbing. It is no surprise that he should
have come finally to include most writers, publishers, and critics
in the circle of the pretentious and snobbish. When he is not rail-
ing against them, he simply keeps quiet. His real love, he declares
over and over again, is the out-of-doors. Compared to the jockey's
glorious ride, an author's trade is a contemptible thing. One of his
biographers relates how he once refused to meet a Russian scholar
"simply because he moved in the literary world." [6]

Borrow's reading habits, combined with his perversity, resulted
in some curious literary judgments. His father was once horrified
to hear George's law teacher tell how, at a party in his house,
George had behaved well until a man asked him about the Classics. "The boy had the impertinence to say that the classics were
much overvalued, and amongst other things that some horrible
fellow or other, some Welshman I think (thank God it was not an
Irishman), was a better poet than Ovid" (*Lavengro*, I, 211). The
poet was Ab Gwylim, a Welshman whom Borrow believed to be
worth half a dozen Chaucers. Or perhaps the enthusiasm was
partly pose, since so few could talk intelligently of Ab Gwylim
that Borrow had the field to himself.

Despite such eccentricities, some influences upon Borrow's

work are easily discernible. The influence of Defoe, especially through *Robinson Crusoe*, would be clear even without Borrow's frequent, eulogistic mention of man and book. And Borrow's consuming interest in the picaresque tradition led him to read with enjoyment other Englishmen who knew and used it. Fielding, Smollett, and Sterne all left their marks upon him. Bunyan's vigorous prose and personal determination appealed to Borrow and without doubt affected his style, although he lacked Bunyan's single-minded moral earnestness. Bunyan's deeply religious mind turned every experience into allegory; Borrow liked adventure so much for its own sake that he had a hard time remembering to tack on the proper moral coda at the end of a narrative. Finally, he could hardly have escaped being influenced in some way by Dickens, whose popularity was enormous during Borrow's early maturity. Dickens' fondness for narratives of low life and his creation of eccentric characters were both sure to appeal to Borrow. Other influences have been cited, but these are the significant ones and the nature of their contribution is worth tracing further.

I *Defoe*

After the Bible, the first book which deeply fascinated Borrow was *Robinson Crusoe*. Ingenuity in distress, the theme of that book, is the motif Borrow enjoyed most in his own narratives. He consciously imitated Defoe; in a letter of 1844 he says he is at work on "a kind of biography in the Robinson Crusoe style." [7] The biography, of course, was *Lavengro*. In the Defoe manner, Borrow takes a real voyage, fills it in with invented incidents, and leaves the reader uncertain as to proportions of fact and fiction. The exact amount of truth in *Lavengro* and in *The Romany Rye* can probably never be ascertained, but no one seriously questions that they are romanticized and that events have been much elaborated, if not completely invented. As Defoe had used the Alexander Selkirk narrative for a framework, then spread over it the fictions his mind invented, so Borrow used his travels as the framework for incidents which readers increasingly disbelieve as truth; and they delight in the fiction as the account progresses. William Dean Howells thought that in the use of this technique Borrow was "so superlatively master as to seem sole in it after Defoe." [8]

The Disciple

The minute realism of Defoe appealed to Borrow. Defoe insisted upon the appearance of veracity, using every technique he knew for the purpose. He builds up his impressive passages by painstakingly accumulating a mountain of prosaic data. He is fond of dropping some comment which the reader will suppose could never occur to a writer in a moment of passion unless it was true. No other reason appears for putting it where it is, except that it has the countenance of truth and demands inclusion. By it, the reader's faith in the accuracy of the narrative is enlarged, and he is prepared to accept the larger statements. Defoe uses this device effectively in his account of the plague year, as well as in many other narratives. An example in Borrow may be found in the second chapter of *Lavengro* where, among all the exciting details of the viper story, the author casually recalls "a frightened hen clucking under the bushes." The unexpected small detail makes the strange story seem credible.

Like Defoe, Borrow knew that, if a thing is to be believed, it must resemble true history. This conviction causes him to write as follows: "The picture in question is in the little parish church of San Tome, at the bottom of the aisle, on the left side of the altar" (*The Bible*, II, 112). The scene may shift next to a wild, dark wood and the deeds of the most extraordinary men; but the reader is ready to believe an author so careful of unimportant facts. It is a great help, of course, to be a chronicler of travels. As one critic says, it is the looseness of organization which gives Borrow wide latitude of subject and "strengthens the Defoe-like illusion of truth; he never loses the tone of the veracious chronicler who put things down in the order of nature and not according to the design of art." [9] The debt to Defoe at this point was considerable.

Borrow undoubtedly responded to Defoe's fascination with the ingenious rogue. In *The Life, Adventures and Pyracies of the Famous Captain Singleton* (1720), Defoe's hero is kidnapped as a child and eventually becomes, for a time, the property of a gypsy. He is one of the cleverest of Defoe characters. And Roxana ingeniously works her way to the top through exploiting a succession of lovers. It is true that neither Defoe nor Borrow was ever quite so much concerned with conscious social exposé as was their mutual idol, Le Sage; but they used eagerly the biographical pattern, the episodic structure, and the protagonist whose wit saved him as he moved from one level of society to another.

Like Borrow, Defoe got much of his knowledge of human nature from his work as a journalist. Through his connection with John Appleby, editor of the *Original Weekly Journal*, he printed the confessions and dying speeches of criminals. His sketches of Jack Sheppard and Jonathan Wild anticipate Borrow's treatment of criminals. Defoe's singular calmness as he describes his villains and their deeds is a characteristic which Borrow imitated to the dismay of some of his more conventional friends.

Not that Defoe could not preach. He slid into sermonic platitudes frequently, echoing the ethics and morals of his own middle-class Protestant world. He yielded to the temptation to make the third volume of the Crusoe tales a moralizing treatise, just as Borrow later was to tack on his frequent moral tags and finally climax the habit with the Appendix to *The Romany Rye*. Both men shift ground so frequently, depending on which stance seems to promise greatest rewards, that one can hardly avoid thinking that their moralizing is generally a sop thrown to a pious audience. The anti-Catholic bias of both often seems more expedient than sincere. When Defoe blasted the sharp trading practices of foreigners, he happily noted that they were Catholics as well as shysters. The path was one which Borrow followed zealously some one hundred years later.

Borrow's principal debts to Defoe may be summed up as follows: he profited from Defoe's skill in characterization; he exploited the episodic technique which Defoe had handled so masterfully; he followed the pattern of the fictional autobiography which exhausts the techniques of verisimilitude in order to convince the reader of its truthfulness; he used the motif of the wandering rogue; and he profited from his study of Defoe's plain, straightforward prose. One who wishes to pursue the subject further than this would do well to begin with Arthur W. Secord's *Studies in the Narrative Method of Defoe* (1924).

II *Fielding*

Borrow also admired Henry Fielding. He mentions him in the same breath with Shakespeare and tells how he kissed the tomb

of this "most singular genius" which the English had produced
(*The Bible*, II, 6). Fielding's contempt for many aspects of aristocratic life and his conviction that virtue is of value only as it sallies
out upon the road to be tested find reflection in Borrow's books. It
may also be true that Borrow learned from Fielding how effective
bursts of eloquence can be in a narrative of constant movement
from place to place. Whether the little chats with the reader
which both men indulged in can be called a Borrow indebtedness
is uncertain; they are common in the literature of the times and
Fielding's use probably only helped confirm Borrow's inclination.

Much more important is the fact that Fielding exhibits many of
the elements of the picaresque tradition. His Parson Adams is
reminiscent of Don Quixote. Adams, a scholarly dreamer, gets
knocked about outrageously but never loses his essential dignity.
He is that curious perversion of the picaresque tradition, the
righteous rogue, the vagabond of God, who takes to the road and
triumphs through a combination of his wits and his Master's (occasional) help. Borrow follows this motif precisely as he writes of
his colportage in Spain. He is another holy rogue intent on doing good, but aware like Parson Adams that this occasionally calls
for outwitting the other fellow and even taking advantage of him.

Borrow's technique of letting dialogue reveal character has
been commented upon elsewhere. How much he may have owed
to Fielding, who developed the art skillfully, is conjectural. Need-
less to say, Borrow never learned the intricacies of plotting, or the
understanding of psychology, which Fielding displays in *Tom
Jones*.

III Smollett

Smollett exercised a similar fascination over Borrow, and for
the same reason. Creator of picaresque heroes, Smollett praised
Cervantes and admits in his preface to *Roderick Random* that he
had been inspired by Le Sage's *Gil Blas*, whom Borrow was to
praise so highly later. Of Borrow's knowledge of Roderick Random and Peregrine Pickle there can be no doubt; he praises them
highly in the first chapter of his Appendix to *The Romany Rye*.
He chose to ignore the uninhibited naughtiness in Smollett and
affixed such adjectives as "moral" and "estimable" to the heroes

named above. But Smollett knew how to write superb episodes and to create memorable travelers, and Borrow must have picked up a trick here and there from one of his favorites.

IV   *Sterne*

From Sterne come some mechanical tricks. Borrow ends many of his chapters with disconcerting abruptness.[10] At the end of Chapter 38 of *Lavengro,* a sentence, abruptly introduced, reads: "Italy—what was I going to say about Italy?" and the next chapter begins with an entirely different subject. Borrow also uses some of Sterne's maddening dots and dashes, a fact remarked on in a 1939 review of one of the Borrow biographes.[11] In his air of mystery, his occasional melting into bathos, and his mechanical quirks, there is certainly something of the willful manner of Sterne. William Dean Howells thought both willful, but that Sterne's willfulness grew out of affectation, while Borrow's grew out of perversity.[12] The judgment seems sound. Sterne's infinite capacity for digressions doubtless justified Borrow's own bent, and Sterne's fondness for military metaphors as a result of his early years in camps and barracks touched an especially receptive nerve in Borrow.

V   *Dickens and Others*

It seems impossible to get far away from the picaresque tradition in a review of writers who influenced Borrow. Charles Dickens, one of the select company whom Borrow praised, had his David Copperfield list the books he had read as a boy. Smollett's *Roderick Random, Peregrine Pickle,* and *Humphrey Clinker* come first; Fielding's *Tom Jones* and Defoe's *Robinson Crusoe* are close behind. Of non-English books, *Don Quixote* and *Gil Blas* are important. That the list reflects Dickens' own taste is likely. *Gil Blas* had been one of his favorites as a boy, and he carries out many of the motifs of the picaresque romance as he follows his titular heroes through the vicissitudes of life. His Pickwick is a member of that great family of characters who get booted about because of naïveté, but who never lose faith or dignity.

At the time of Borrow's early success, England was in the Pickwick fever. Borrow calls Dickens "a second Fielding" and with his customary egotism speaks of the "humour, variety and profound knowledge of character" which charm readers, "at least those who have the capacity to understand him." [13] He relates that upon his arrival in London in 1838 "everybody was in raptures over a certain *Oliver Twist* that had just come out, and the *Memoirs of the Nickleby Family*, which was appearing in fortnightly numbers." He was "delighted with them, especially with *Oliver Twist*." [14]

Dickens' predilection for writing about odd, distorted, memorable characters must have impressed Borrow. He employs throughout his own books the Dickensian devices of caricature. The metallic quality of Miss Murdstone, the way Peggotty's buttons are forever flying off, these are reminiscent of Borrow's dwarf guide in his Spanish adventure story and of Lavengro's "Long Melford" or right-fisted blow in the battle with the Flaming Tinman. Borrow himself, of course, is bizarre enough to have walked out of the pages of Dickens and one suspects he may have emphasized his own eccentricities a bit now and then after having rejoiced so much in those of Dickens' characters.

There may also be a touch of Scott and of Bunyan. Scott certainly had tastes which Borrow found congenial. The love of curious old books about ancient and northern things is a good example. And the "wild sublimity" which Scott says Meg Merrilees had sounds much like Borrow's Isopel Berners. Borrow knew Meg, because he laughed at Scott's gypsy language in parts of *Guy Mannering*. That novel and *Quentin Durward* feature the gypsy characters to whom Borrow was to devote himself. Borrow ultimately came to detest Scott, laying the whole blame for the Oxford Movement upon his shoulders; but he must have been encouraged by his fellow author in the writing of romantic adventure and in the idealization of the past.

The strong antipathies and great enthusiasms of Bunyan, with the unschooled tinker's religious fervor and King James style, all left echoes which sound now strongly, now faintly through the Borrow canon. But Borrow's deepest love was for the open road and vagabondage; his spirit was never so subdued to Christian loyalties as was Bunyan's. What seems clearest in a survey of literary influences is that Borrow was most strongly swayed by those writers who shared broad human experience, had been themselves profoundly affected by the picaresque novels of Le Sage and Cervantes, and who found some way to make the adventures of the common man seem exciting and significant. In their company Borrow belongs.

CHAPTER 6

The Teacher

TRACES of George Borrow's influence upon other writers are not hard to find. His fascination with gypsies stimulated interest in that subject in both England and America, provoking books and articles. Perhaps the most representative novel in this class is Theodore Watts-Dunton's *Aylwin* (1898). Other authors who appreciated Borrow's wanderings and his delight in physical prowess, but who did not share his interest in gypsies, composed episodes strikingly reminiscent of some of Borrow's creations. Not surprisingly, the most memorable of all single episodes in Borrow's novels has been the Mumper's Dingle interlude, in which the hero camps in a dell with statuesque Isopel Berners and avoids romantic entanglements by teaching her Armenian. Two early twentieth-century novels imitated this tale closely, including its famous fistfight and the quixotic character of its hero.

Jeffery Farnol follows the pattern of Borrow's narrative so closely in his novel *The Broad Highway* (1911) that it seems unquestionably to have been influenced by the *Lavengro-Romany Rye* accounts. His hero is reminiscent of Lavengro in physical agility and mental skills. Like Lavengro, he pauses in his wanderings to settle temporarily in a lovely dell where he works at the smith's trade. A young woman named Charmian, handsome and mysterious like Isopel, appears. She is followed by a villain whom the hero must vanquish. In the fight, the villain strikes his head against a stone in falling, permitting the hero to win. Lavengro, it will be recalled, won his epic fight with the Flaming Tinman only after that worthy had missed with a prodigious blow and struck a tree trunk with his fist. The hero and the girl in Farnol's book live in the dingle for a time, during which he plagues her with his learning, just as Lavengro had pestered Isopel with the grammar lessons. Farnol improves on Borrow by presenting two fistfights rather than one. He even has a postillion appear, just as one had appeared in the dell in *Lavengro*.

The Borrow atmosphere is struck immediately in Farnol's novel. His narrator sits in the shade of a tree eating fried bacon with a tinker as the story begins. He decides to write "a book that should treat of the roads and by-roads, of trees, and wind in lonely places, of rapid brooks and lazy streams, of the glory of dawn, the glow of evening, and the purple solitude of night; a book of way-side inns and sequestered taverns; a book of country things and ways and people." [1] The tinker doubts that people would enjoy a book about a tinker. He says that he never read a novel with a tinker in it, that "they're generally dooks, or earls, or barronites— nobody wants to read about a tinker." [2] But Farnol had clearly read about them, for they appear repeatedly in his novels.

Nina Wilcox Putman's *In Search of Arcady* (1912) also uses a dingle episode which seems too much like Borrow's to be coinci-dental. She presents a robust, wandering hero who purchases a chair-peddler's equipment and makes camp in scenic places with a girl like Belle. Thought to be a gypsy, she sells gewgaws from a cart; Belle had done this in Borrow's story. An epic fistfight occurs when the hero meets a huge gypsy who looks and fights like Bor-row's Flaming Tinman. Once again the hero wins the fight by taking advantage of his opponent's accidental discomfiture; this time the villain slips. In Miss Putnam's novel, as in Farnol's, the hero knocks his foe unconscious.

Farnol pursued other Borrow themes in succeeding novels. In *The Amateur Gentleman* (1913) he opens with his hero having to knock down his father, an ex-champion boxer. The hero does so gently, regretfully, but effectively. Like Borrow's Lavengro he is not a gentleman born, but a true one despite his lineage. The book reflects Borrow's passionate belief that the true aristocracy of England was not to be found in famous genealogies.

In *Beltane the Smith* (1915) Farnol presents a mighty hero who lives in a forest glade but who knows the courses of the stars and is versed in ancient philosophies. He has learned both Latin and Greek from Ambrose the Hermit. He knows nothing of the ways of women; but, unlike Borrow's autobiographical heroes, he remedies this deficiency. Farnol often strains for effect and his exoticism palls. Commenting on such novels, Homer Woodbridge said: "Like Borrow's story as they are, however, in situation, they are at the opposite pole from it in style and tone. Instead of the square-cut sentences of Borrow, we find in the recent stories a somewhat mincing and elaborate affectation of style." [3]

There can be little doubt about the degree of Borrow's influence upon his admirer, Theodore Watts-Dunton, whose romantic novel, *Aylwin*, created a temporary sensation at the end of the nineteenth century. The gypsy lore in this novel is a legacy from Borrow's own vast enthusiasm for the subject. The book stimulated an open-air cult which had sprung up in the late nineteenth century and which lasted a decade into the twentieth.

Although *Aylwin* would almost certainly not have been written except for Borrow's earlier successes, there is a great difference in treatment between it and the *Lavengro-Romany Rye* combination. Borrow was basically a Realist who appears to have decided, quite deliberately, that he would touch gypsy life with romance. Watts-Dunton, on the other hand, is basically a Romanticist whose gypsies never seem quite true. One is left with the sense that they have been strained through the sieve of Watts-Dunton's own idealism. Lacking the amorality and aberrations of Borrow's gypsies, they lack also the color and vitality of their predecessors. Not a single one of them spends time in justifying in racy prose the arts of beating, cheating, scheming, and killing. It is true that such things occur in *Aylwin* (Rhoma, married to Percy Aylwin, is killed by her angry tribe, for example); but, unlike Borrow, Watts-Dunton does not pause to examine the strange, twisted logic the gypsies would have used to justify their action. Borrow's roguery, his picaresque feeling for the romance of the real, is lost; a Romantic idealism appears instead.

It is not possible to trace Borrow's influence so directly upon Maurice Hewlett, but his trilogy (*Halfway House*, 1908; *Open Country*, 1908; *Rest Harrow*, 1910) features a wandering philosopher named Jack Senhouse who reminds one of Lavengro in his strenuous quest for independence and in his eccentricities. He will neither own property nor live under a roof, and he is happiest when he is travelling about the country mending manners and impressing strangers with his philosophy. The heroine of the series is Sanchia-Josepha, a delightful woman who deserves to be properly married by the hero but who, like Isopel Berners, is put off from this happy consummation by the idiosyncrasies of her beloved.

Hewlett's manner of handling historical stories is reminiscent of Borrow's. He is true not to the actual facts of his tale but to the spirit of its time and place. His book *The Queen's Quair* (1904) is, like *The Bible in Spain*, truer than literal travelogue reporting could have been. It may be due partly to Borrow's influence that Hewlett wrote a pair of picaresque stories, *The Fool Errant* (1905) and *Brazenhead the Great* (1911). Ernest Baker finds "a dash of George Borrow" also in Hewlett's *Mrs. Lancelot* (1912).[4]

Other writers seem to have profited either from Borrow's subject matter or from his style. In his *Essays of Travel*, Robert Louis Stevenson listed as one of those books that do not grow stale, *The Bible in Spain*. A student of the English novel believes that the incidents Stevenson created follow in the footsteps of Borrow, among others.[5] His first book, *An Inland Voyage* (1878), and his second, *Travels with a Donkey* (1879), show Bohemian touches reminiscent of Borrow.

Stories of criminal lives, popular in England from about 1773 when *The Newgate Calendar* was published in five volumes, owe a debt to Borrow. He had published his own *Celebrated Trials and Remarkable Cases of Criminal Jurisprudence from the Earliest Records to the Year of 1825*, without his name, in 1825. Borrow's style was so vivid that his book added new impetus to an already-popular genre. Some of the criminal types and their psychologies appear in partial disguise throughout Borrow's later books. Readers interested in the development of what has been called the Newgate novel may consult a recent study of the type.[6]

Traces of discernible Borrow influence grow thin as one proceeds. Ernest Baker says of William Henry Hudson (1841-1922) that "He read Dickens: but it is the alert eye of Borrow for grotesque and astonishing character that might have caught the outward features of such a procession as the lad's schoolmaster Mr. Trigg and his successor Father O'Keefe, Zango the old horse and the dog Caesar, Barboza the fighter and Jack the killer, Don Evaristo and his six wives, and the dictator Rosas, 'The Tiger of Palermo,' his fool Eusebio and the traitor Urquiza."[7] In one of George Meredith's books, *Adventures of Harry Richmond* (1897), there is a gypsy girl who reminds readers faintly of Isopel Berners.

The Teacher

She exchanges blows with Meredith's hero, just as Isopel had once done in the dingle with Lavengro.

Many other writers were probably influenced by the open-air cult who never read Borrow directly but were indoctrinated second-hand by some disciple. It is even more likely that most treatments of gypsy life after Borrow's time owed something to his manner of handling them. It may be true that if "Borrow had ever seen a real gypsy he would have died of fright"; but, like a great many persuasive fictions, Borrow's handling of the gypsy themes caught and held public fancy despite the later protests against his accuracy.[8] Certainly Borrow had satisfied the nomadic impulses which drive countless readers to fiction, and careful craftsmen would not fail to observe his techniques. Sherwood Anderson found merit in Borrow's stylistic devices and advised a friend to read Borrow to learn the tricks of the trade.[9] Beyond such traces one may not safely go.

CHAPTER 7

Conclusion

W HAT is clearest, perhaps, after an analysis of Borrow's prose style is that it remains singularly his own despite the traces of indebtedness. The peculiar combination of merits and defects, of careful verisimilitude and awkward inconsistency, of racy, vivid prose and ponderous deadwood, does indeed give him a unique charm. His greatest admirers have not been blind to the flaws; one of the most ardent of them, Whitworth Elwin, manfully confessed that "there is but one step from exquisite simplicity to insipidity, and the flaw in Borrow is that he frequently crossed the line which divides them." [1] But they have discovered such delights that they do not care, arguing that "those who have once come under his spell" tend to "listen unmoved to the adverse criticism which indeed he often fully merited." [2]

Readers not so completely surrendered, however, may see some irony in Borrow's own pronouncement upon the subject of his future reputation: "Yes, I think I may promise myself a reputation of a thousand years if I do but give myself the necessary trouble" (*Lavengro*, I, 267). Forgotten in his own lifetime and neglected until the resolute Borrovians brought him briefly back to prominence early in the present century, Borrow lives today only feebly. No sudden renovation of his fame seems likely, although a dedicated few persist and wide-ranging readers occasionally stumble upon his books with delight. Even students of the craft of fiction have refused to credit Borrow with having taken "the necessary trouble," despite the persuasiveness of two excellent articles on his literary artistry by a capable modern critic. [3]

But the charm remains, imbedded in Borrow's generally shapeless books. And it is so unmistakably his own that it lends itself easily to that sometime tribute to genius, the parody. It may be fitting that here, at the end of thematic and stylistic examination, a brilliant burlesque of Borrow's mannerisms should provide for us a different kind of criticism. The student who has bothered to read even one Borrow book before coming to this study will have no difficulty appreciating the parody. It appears in a chapter entitled, "Borrowed Scenes," where Arthur Conan Doyle pretends to become George Borrow engaged in narration:

As I walked, I entertained myself by recollections of the founders of Sussex, of Cerdic that mighty sea-rover, and of Ella his son, said by the bard to be taller by the length of a spear-head than the tallest of his fellows. I mentioned the matter twice to peasants whom I met upon the road. One, a tallish man with a freckled face, sidled past me and ran swiftly towards the station. The other, a smaller and older man, stood entranced while I recited to him that passage of the Saxon Chronicle which begins, 'Then came Leija with long-hips forty-four, and the fyrd went out against him.' I was pointing out to him that the Chronicle had been written partly by the monks of Saint Alban's and afterwards by those of Peterborough, but the fellow sprang suddenly over a gate and disappeared.

The village of Swinehurst is a straggling line of half-timbered houses of the early English pattern. One of these houses stood, as I observed, somewhat taller than the rest, and seeing by its appearance and by the sign which hung before it that it was the village inn, I approached it, for indeed I had not broken my fast since I had left London. A stoutish man, five foot eight perhaps in height, with black coat and trousers of a greyish shade, stood outside, and to him I walked in the fashion of the master.

"Why a rose and why a crown?" I asked as I pointed upwards.

He looked at me in a strange manner. The man's whole appearance was strange. "Why not?" he answered, and shrank a little backwards.

"The sign of a king," said I.

"Surely," said he. "What else should we understand from a crown?"

"And which king?" I asked.

"You will excuse me," said he, and tried to pass.

"Which king?" I repeated.

"How should I know?" he asked.

"You should know by the rose," said I, "which is the symbol of that Tudor-ap-Tudor, who, coming from the mountains of Wales, yet seated his posterity upon the English throne. Tudor," I continued, getting between the stranger and the door of the inn, through which he appeared to be desirous of passing, "was of the same blood as Owen Glendower, the famous chieftain, who is by no means to be confused with the Owen Gwynedd, the father of Madoc of the Sea, of whom the bard made the famous cnylyn, which runs in the Welsh as follows:—"

I was about to repeat the famous stanza of Dafydd-ap-Gwilyn when the man, who had looked very fixedly and strangely at me as I spoke, pushed past me and entered the inn. "Truly," said I aloud, "it is surely Swinehurst to which I have come, since the same means the grove of the hogs." [4]

This captures so many of the essential ingredients of Borrow's style, and even of his personality, that it would require countless pages of illustration to demonstrate to the non-reader of Borrow how clever it is. Viewed simply as parody, it is much superior to Scott's well-known burlesque of euphuistic style in *The Monastery*, where he misses some of the most conspicuous features. It mimics devastatingly Borrow's interest in ancient history and myth, especially that of the north; and it satirizes effectively his zeal for exhibiting his linguistic skill, even if the audience must be held captive while he does it. But there are milder Borrow touches which it misses and which might appropriately be printed here for the reader who has no easy access to Borrow's writings. The following passage has more typical Borrow mannerisms:

On the fifth day, about two o'clock, I arrived at a small town. Feeling hungry, I entered a decent-looking inn. Within a kind of bar I saw a huge, fat, landlord-looking person, with a very pretty, smartly dressed maiden. Addressing myself to the fat man, "House!" said I, "house! Can I have dinner, house?"

"Young gentleman," said the huge, fat landlord, "you are come at the right time; dinner will be taken up in a few minutes, and such a dinner," he continued, rubbing his hands, "as you will not see every day in these times."

"I am hot and dusty," said I, "and should wish to cool my hands and face."

"Jenny!" said the huge landlord, with the utmost gravity, "show the gentleman into number seven, that he may wash his hands and face."

"By no means," said I; "I am a person of primitive habits, and there is nothing like the pump in weather like this."

"Jenny!" said the landlord, with the same gravity as before, "go with the young gentleman to the pump in the back kitchen, and take a clean towel along with you."

[134]

Conclusion

Thereupon the rosy-faced, clean-looking damsel went to a drawer, and, producing a large, thick, but snowy-white towel, she nodded to me to follow her through a long passage into the back kitchen.

And at the end of the back kitchen there stood a pump; and going to it I placed my hands beneath the spout, and said, "Pump, Jenny," and Jenny incontinently, without laying down the towel, pumped with one hand, and I washed and cooled my heated hands.

And, when my hands were washed and cooled, I took off my neck-cloth, and, unbuttoning my shirt collar, I placed my head beneath the spout of the pump, and I said unto Jenny: "Now, Jenny, lay down the towel, and pump for your life."

Thereupon Jenny, placing the towel on a linen-horse, took the handle of the pump with both hands and pumped over my head as hand-maid had never pumped before; so that the water poured in torrents from my head, my face, and my hair down upon the brick floor.

And after the lapse of somewhat more than a minute, I called out with a half-strangled voice, "Hold, Jenny!" and Jenny desisted. I stood for a few moments to recover my breath, then, taking the towel which Jenny proffered, I dried composedly my hands, and head, my face and hair; then, returning the towel to Jenny, I gave a deep sigh and said: "Surely this is one of the pleasant moments of life."

(*Lavengro*, II, 83-85)

Here is the wry, grave humor, the racy narration, the interwoven Biblical diction and rhythms, and the unmistakable stamp of Borrow's flamboyant personality. This domestic and trivial moment is touched with inexplicable charm. The curious Borrow ability to make something of nothing is here. The extract may appropriately stand as an epilogue to our study, in which the student of Borrow may see again a great many of his author's stylistic mannerisms, and in which the non-reader of Borrow may find as fair a sample of this quirky Englishman's charm as he is likely to come upon anywhere outside the books themselves.

Notes and References

Chapter One

1. William I. Knapp, *Life, Writings and Correspondence of George Borrow* (1899), I, 379. Knapp's two-volume work provides more purely factual data about Borrow than any other study.
2. April 24, 1841, p. 318.
3. Sept., 1841, p. 362.
4. June, 1842, p. 415.
5. Knapp regretted that Ford's criticism did not come soon enough to improve Borrow's first book, but it "was already written, and therefore could not partake of the wisdom of the master-hand" (Knapp, I, 378). For examples of the kind of criticism Ford made, see Knapp, I, 378-86.
6. Stuart Northam's unpublished doctoral dissertation, "An Analysis of the Methods of Fiction Used by George Borrow" (Denver University, 1954), explores extensively the techniques Borrow used in composing *The Bible in Spain* and notes that the author was not slavishly dependent upon the Bible Society letters.
7. The forty and fifty thousand purchasers of *Pickwick* and *Nickleby*, the sixty and seventy thousands of the early numbers of the *Old Curiosity Shop* and *Barnaby Rudge*, had fallen to "only a little over 20,000 copies a number," according to Arthur Waugh. Waugh's book *A Hundred Years of Publishing* (1930), p. 59, discusses the alarm of Dickens' publishers over this slump. Several studies of Dickens testify to the momentary lull in Dickens' popularity around 1843-44. It was a happy accident for Borrow.
8. *Athenaeum*, May 27, 1843, p. 511.
9. Dec. 31, 1842, p. 1131.
10. Mar. 1843, p. 174.
11. Knapp, I, 398-401.
12. June, 1843, p. 321.
13. *Dublin University Magazine*, Jan.-June, 1843, p. 265.
14. *Stones From a Glass House* (1904), p. 156.
15. *Res Judicatae* (1892), p. 137.

16. *Harper's Magazine*, Nov. 1914, p. 959.
17. P. 172.
18. *Athenaeum*, July 8, 1893, p. 65.
19. *Op. cit.*, p. 177.
20. *London Times*, April 12, 1843. Peel admitted the difficulties connected with getting a bishopric in Jerusalem, but reminded his hearers that "If Mr. Borrow had been deterred by trifling obstacles, the circulation of the Bible in Spain would never have been advanced to the extent which has happily attained. If he had not persevered he would not have been the agent of so much enlightenment." Borrow complained that the newspapers had not reported Sir Robert's speech completely and urged Murray to make use of it when he advertised the fourth edition of *Zincali* (Knapp, II, 325).
21. June, 1851, p. 393.
22. June, 1853, pp. 363, 377.
23. Feb. 8, 1851, p. 159.
24. May 23, 1857, pp. 480-81.
25. May 23, 1857, p. 653.
26. Jan., 1863, p. 137.
27. *Athenaeum*, Mar. 17, 1888, p. 340.

Chapter Two

1. It is almost a literal impossibility to leaf through a major British periodical between 1840 and 1860 without coming upon a review or a notice of publication of some travel narrative.
2. These famous travel narratives were published during Borrow's formative years: Thomas Hope's *Anastasius, or Memoirs of a Greek* (1819); James Morier's *Hajji Baba of Ispahan* (1824) and a sequel, *Hajji Baba in London* (1828); Edward John Trelawny's *Adventures of a Younger Son* (1831); and, just before the publication of Borrow's first travel tale, Frederick Marryat's *Mr. Midshipman Easy* (1836) and *Masterman Ready* (1841).
3. According to William I. Knapp, *Life, Writings and Correspondence of George Borrow* (1899), I, 387, Ford had written such advice during the composition of *The Bible in Spain*.
4. *Views and Reviews* (1890), p. 135.
5. *A Short History of English Literature* (1927), p. 792.
6. *A History of English Literature* (1950), p. 562.
7. *Hello, Towns!* (1929), p. 31. Anderson will seem extraordinarily wrong to many readers.
8. *Harper's* (Nov., 1914), p. 958.
9. *A History of English Literature* (1953), p. 553. Clement Shorter, *George Borrow and His Circle* (1913), p. 136, says that Borrow's as-

sertion that he had "visited most of the principal capitals of the world" would be called a "palpable lie were not so much of *The Bible in Spain* sheer invention." Rudolph Scheville, *University of California Chronicle* (Jan., 1916), p. 1, calls the book "a most brilliant and melodramatic mixture of truth and buncombe."

10. Frank Beck, *Methodist Review* (May, 1916), p. 441, calls Borrow "the head and chief of the picaresque school. It might not be too bold to say that he is the one true poet of them all." In *Quarterly Review* (March, 1843), p. 172, Richard Ford echoed many others when he said "we are more frequently reminded of *Gil Blas,* in the narratives of this pious single-hearted man, than in the perusal of almost any modern novelist's pages."

11. Rene Wellek and Austin Warren, *Theory of Literature* (1942), p. 222.

12. (1907), II, 445.

13. *Res Judicatae* (1892), p. 126.

14. *Edinburgh Review* (April, 1843), p. 112.

15. Edward Thomas, *George Borrow: The Man and His Books* (1912), p. 300.

16. Mr. Brandram, secretary of the Society, rebuked Borrow for speaking of his "usual wonderful good fortune." Said Brandram: "This is a mode of speaking to which we are not well accustomed; it savours, some of our friends would say, a little of the profane" (Knapp, I, 313-14, quoting a letter of May 22, 1839).

The Reverend Joseph Jowett had warned Borrow several years earlier in a letter of July 5, 1833, while Borrow was still in England hoping for a missionary journey:

"Excuse me if, as a clergyman, and your senior in years though not in talent, I venture, with the kindest of motives, to throw out a hint which may not be without its use. I am sure you will not be offended if I suggest that there is occasionally a tone of confidence in speaking of yourself, which has alarmed some of the excellent members of our Committee. It may have been this feeling, more than once displayed before, which prepared one or two of them to stumble at an expression in your letter of yesterday, in which, till pointed out, I confess I was not struck with anything objectionable, but at which, nevertheless, a humble Christian might not unreasonably take umbrage. It is where you speak of the prospect of becoming *'useful to the Deity, to man, and to yourself.'* Doubtless you meant, *the prospect of glorifying God;* but the turn of expression made us think of such passages of Scripture as Job xxi.2; xxxv.7 and 8; Psalm xvi.2 and 3" (Knapp, I, 161).

17. Thurston Hopkins, *George Borrow* (1922), pp. 88-89.

18. *George Borrow* (1950), p. 21. Armstrong's approach is psychoanalytical. He thinks Borrow is a case for Freudian analysis, and does some of the job himself.

19. Knapp, II, 285.

20. *United States Catholic Magazine* (June, 1843), p. 322. The citation is from *The Bible in Spain*, II, 238.

21. *Athenaeum* (Sept. 10, 1881), p. 336. Watts-Dunton said: "His unswerving belief in the beneficence of God was most beautiful—most touching."

22. *The Bible*, I, 271. Similar references to Providence occur in *The Bible*, II, 106 and *Romany Rye*, II, 196.

23. Amy Cruse, *The Victorians and Their Reading* (1935), p. 80. She adds that the book's "popularity lasted for at least fifty years." Clement Shorter, *George Borrow and His Circle* (1913), p. 97, says the book "sold in hundreds of thousands, and is still much prized by the Evangelical folk who buy the publications of the Religious Tract Society."

24. Harriet Martineau was one. She said of Borrow: "When this polyglot gentleman appeared before the public as a devout agent of the Bible-Society in foreign parts, there was one burst of laughter from all who remembered the old Norwich days." *Autobiography*, ed. Maria Chapman (1877), I, 227. Bad blood between Borrow and the Martineau family makes the objectivity of this comment slightly suspect.

Borrow probably refers to the Norwich days, perhaps to William Taylor in particular, when he says: "For a long time I doubted the truth of Scripture, owing to certain conceited discourses which I heard from certain conceited individuals, but now I begin to believe firmly" (*Romany Rye*, I, 37).

25. Byron chose sham and pretense; Borrow, above all else, chose Catholicism. Both of them dedicated the rest of their lives to fighting their particular *bête noire* in whatever form it appeared.

26. All Borrow's biographers comment upon his restlessness and increasing boorishness after he settled down with his wife at Oulton. For the fullest discussion, see Herbert Jenkins, *George Borrow* (1924), Chap. 29.

27. John Macy, *The Critical Game* (1922), p. 255.

28. *Encyclopaedia Britannica*, Eleventh Edition, Vols. III-IV, p. 275.

29. *Quarterly Review* (March, 1843), p. 171.

30. *Athenaeum* (Aug. 13, 1881), p. 209.

31. *Ibid.*, (Sept. 3, 1881), p. 307.

32. Sept. 17, 1853. Under a heading of "Intrepidity," the paper gave this account: "Yarmouth jetty presented an extraordinary and thrilling spectacle on Thursday, the 8th inst., about one o'clock. The sea raged

frantically, and a ship's boat, endeavoring to land for water, was upset, and the men were engulfed in a wave some thirty feet high, and struggling with it in vain. The moment was an awful one, when George Borrow, the well-known author of *Lavengro,* and *The Bible in Spain,* dashed into the surf and saved one life, and through his instrumentality the others were saved. We ourselves have known this brave and gifted man for years, and, daring as was this deed, we have known him more than once to risk his life for others." The article was copied by the press all over England, appearing on the 20th of that month in the *Plymouth Mail* under the heading, "Gallant Conduct of Mr. G. Borrow." (Knapp, II, 72).

33. *Elizabeth Barrett to Miss Mitford,* ed. Betty Miller (1954), p. 182.

34. *Ibid.,* pp. 189-90.

35. Knapp, II, 308.

36. Herbert Jenkins, *George Borrow* (1924), p. 334.

37. *Ibid.,* p. 486.

38. *The Life of George Borrow* (1928), pp. 41, 81.

39. Knapp, I, 371.

40. *Notes and Queries* (Sept. 4, 1926), pp. 165-66.

41. *Letters of Sherwood Anderson,* ed. Howard Mumford Jones (1953), p. 431.

42. *Commonweal* (July 5, 1940), p. 222.

43. (July, 1914), p. 46. Borrow's praise of the "Good Presbyter" (*The Bible,* I, 305) is typical of the compliments the writer has in mind. Borrow found not a few Catholics who seemed to him to lack only the free use of the New Testament to make them perfect.

44. (May, 1843), p. 449.

45. Jenkins, *op. cit.,* p. 382.

46. *Res Judicatae* (1892), p. 115.

47. An excellent account of the Cult may be had in an unpublished doctoral dissertation. Troy C. Crenshaw, "George Borrow and the Borrovian Cult," University of Texas, 1937, names Birrell as the first to use the phrase, in 1893. Others who devoted their energies to eulogizing the gypsy author were the Reverend Whitwell Elwin, A. Egmont Hake, Theodore Watts-Dunton, Augustus Jessop, and Charles Mackie. Typical of their comments are these statements: Jessop, in the *Athenaeum* (July 8, 1893), p. 66, said that Borrow "could touch pitch and not be defiled—walk through the fire and not be burned. Woe to the weak and half-hearted who shall try to pass through such ordeals as George Borrow endured! It is not everyone who can draw Ulysses' bow"; A. Egmont Hake, in the *Athenaeum* (Aug. 13, 1881), p. 209, said that "few men have ever made so deep an impression on me as

George Borrow. His tall, broad figure, his stately bearing, his fine brown eyes, so bright yet soft, his thick white hair, his oval, beardless face, his loud rich voice and bold heroic air were such as to impress the most indifferent of lookers-on."

But the supreme expression of Borrovianism is to be found in these sentences by Thurston Hopkins, *George Borrow, Lord of the Open Road* (1922), pp. 15-16: "George Borrow surpassed anything he ever wrote, and he was always greater than his works. His vivid and abundant personality was too large and generous to be closed within the covers of even such amazing books as *Lavengro* and *The Romany Rye* . . . And the true Borrovian simply loves George Borrow, placing his books entirely out of the question. . . . The mystery of Borrow is itself mysterious."

In the early 1920's, the Borrovian Cult seemed to be reviving. John Macy, *The Critical Game* (1922), p. 253, believed this was because "the cult of the open air has increased." The George Borrow Celebration in Norwich on July 5-6, 1913, reflected this interest. An article in *Nation* (July 24, 1913), p. 30, listed those present (among them, Augustine Birrell, Sir Sidney Lee, and the widow of Dr. Knapp), and said that "while only a frail emphasis was put upon Borrow as the apostle of the open air, it is this doubtless that explains his new clutch upon the hearts of the English world." This flareup among the Borrovians died down after World War II, and there has been no similar revival.

Chapter Three

1. *Views and Reviews, Essays in Appreciation* (1890), p. 137.
2. *Essays in English Literature* (1891), p. 414.
3. *Letters of Sherwood Anderson,* ed. Howard Mumford Jones (1953), p. 431.
4. *Through the Magic Door* (1908), p. 99.
5. Edd Winfield Parks, "Portrait of Lavengro: A Biographical Essay on George Borrow," *Segments of Southern Thought* (1938), p. 99.
6. "George Borrow, Friend of Thinkers and Gypsies," New York *Times Book Review* (Dec. 23, 1923), p. 15. Lionel Johnson once wrote: "Mr. Meredith, Mr. Pater, Mr. Stevenson grew into their styles, finding their way. Borrow seems to have come into the world with his own proper gift of style, so indissolubly wedded to his nature, so inseparable from his themes." *Views and Reviews* (1890), p. 203.
7. August 28, 1924, p. 518.
8. *The Critical Game* (1922), p. 249.
9. *Blackwood's Magazine* (Sept. 10, 1842), pp. 300-1.
10. (1898), p. 3.

Notes and References

11. Quoted in Clement Shorter, *The Life of George Borrow* (1928), p. 269. Shorthouse's dictum is preserved in *Life, Letters and Literary Remains of J. H. Shorthouse* (1905), II, 78.

12. *Wanderings in Spain* (1853), p. 15.

13. *Ibid.*, p. 157.

14. Borrow had been influenced by his compilation *Newgate Lives and Trials*, otherwise known as *Celebrated Trials and Remarkable Cases of Criminal Jurisprudence* . . . , a work he did under the direction of the vegetarian and teetotalling publisher, Sir Richard Phillips, whose mannerisms are so effectively portrayed in *Lavengro*. This task probably helped cause Borrow to look afterwards for the grim aberrations in human conduct; an unusual number of the characters introduced in his narratives are violators of law in some way.

15. When Borrow resolves on occasion to abandon simple narrative of events in sequence and indulge in invention, he sets about it this way: he reintroduces later in his book characters who were mentioned or who had appeared earlier. He does this with Benedict Mol in *The Bible in Spain*, with the old apple-woman and the pick-pocket in *Lavengro*, and with Jasper Petulengro through *Lavengro-The Romany Rye*. The reappearances are highly coincidental and unconvincing, especially since few of the characters are made so real that a return makes any difference to the reader.

16. *Critiques* (1927), p. 117.

17. *Theory of Literature* (1942), pp. 224-25.

18. *Op. cit.*, p. 102.

19. *Hello, Towns!* (1929), p. 137.

20. *The Demon of the Absolute* (1928), p. 139.

21. *Commonweal* (July 5, 1940), p. 222.

22. "Recollections of Early Reading," by a County Magistrate, *Blackwood's Magazine* (Sept. 10, 1842), pp. 300-1, includes this classic example of lush prose: "The slanting rays of the fast-declining sun illuminated with sombre light the shadows cast by the projecting masses of the Appenines across a deep mountain gorge, whose recesses were more intensely darkened by the groves of dark pine-trees, interspersed with wild oaks, which give such an enchanting richness to the landscape of Italy. An eagle, poised high in the air, bore far up on its bright and dazzling wings the full glow of the sunshine, and seemed like a sapphire fixed in the deep blue firmament above, through which came faintly, one by one, the pale stars of evening, and mingled their feeble light with the expiring glories of the great orb of day."

23. *Edinburgh Review* (April, 1843), pp. 114-15.

24. *Lavengro*, I, 119-21; 136-39; II, 68-73.

25. See the unpublished dissertation (University of Texas, 1937) by Troy C. Crenshaw, "George Borrow and the Borrovian Cult," pp. 162--165.

26. *The Bible in Spain*, I, 356; II, 112, 270; *Lavengro*, I, 372-74.

27. William I. Knapp, *Life, Writings and Correspondence of George Borrow* (1899), II, 10.

28. Richard Ford thought Borrow colored "like Rembrandt, and draws like Spagnolette, rather than with the voluptuous sunniness of Claude Lorraine and Albano" (*Edinburgh Review*, April, 1843, p. 114). Philarète Chasles, writing a French review of *The Bible in Spain*, said: "The portraits of bandits, monks, smugglers, bohemians and muleteers, which made up the usual company of the traveler, are worthy of Zurbaran" (*Revue des deux mondes*, May, 1843, p. 401). I recall one place, especially, where Borrow paints a word picture of two young men being executed by strangulation upon a wooden stage and does it in a manner reminiscent of Goya's etchings, in its strong, brilliant and unflinching use of detail. (See *The Bible*, I, 185-86).

29. *Athenaeum* (Sept. 3, 1881), p. 307.

30. *Essays in English Literature* (1891), p. 424. See *Lavengro*, II, 63-66 for an excellent example of the way Borrow characterizes a coachman through description.

31. *The Southern Literary Messenger* (Feb., 1843), p. 481.

32. *The Christian Examiner* (Mar. 17, 1843), p. 171.

33. Feb., 1843, pp. 257-58.

34. *Essays in English Literature*, p. 414.

35. Borrow's publisher, John Murray, handed over the manuscripts to Ford as official reader and critic. Ford frequently commented on the dialogue, saying that "in several of them the tone of the speakers, of those especially who are in humble life, is too correct and elevated, and therefore out of character. This takes away from their effect. I think it would be advisable that Mr. Borrow should go over them with reference to this point, simplifying a few of the turns of expression and introducing a few contractions—don't, can'ts, etc. This would improve them greatly" (Letter quoted in Knapp, I, 384-85). During Borrow's retouching of the book, before final delivery of the manuscript to Murray on Feb. 23, 1842, Ford was writing advice about the dialogue (Knapp, I, 387-88). Borrow profited, although he insisted upon romanticizing the speech of his gypsy characters when he wished to heighten the air of mystery and romance surrounding them.

36. Borrow often tags a speaker by having him repeat a single word like this. A character named Baltasar, for example, talks in this manner: "We send for wine, Don Jorge, and the nationals become wild, Don

Jorge . . ." Wherever he appears, the "Don Jorge" phrase appears with him (*The Bible*, I, 184, 215, 223). The phrase "affairs of Egypt" is repeatedly on Antonio's lips.

37. One may find examples on almost any page in Borrow. Perhaps the best sustained one (embodying French) is in that delightful vignette where Borrow meets Francis Ardry and his flashing-eyed female companion (*Lavengro*, II, 60-61).

38. *Lavengro*, I, 171-72. Borrow skillfully distinguishes on another occasion between the speech of his father and that of his mother (*Lavengro*, I, 212, 221). The long word-groups and military metaphors of his father's talk are delivered with clarity and authority. The mother moves abruptly from one idea to another and at the end jumbles her ideas as if Borrow wanted us to feel in her speech her nervousness. The dialogue of an old ostler in *The Romany Rye* (I, 239-40) is also masterful. The old man's loquaciousness, his pride in his profession, and his total recall are all represented scrupulously.

39. *A Survey of English Literature* (1920), I, 323.

40. *South Atlantic Studies for Sturgis E. Leavitt*, ed. Thomas B. Stroup and Sterling A. Stoudemire (1953), p. 200.

41. *Encyclopaedia Britannica*, Eleventh Edition, II, 275.

42. It is interesting to note that Borrow did not consider his own dialogues inconsistent. In attacking Wordsworth, whose poetry he described as a soporific for the most practiced insomniac, he pounces upon precisely the fault for which he has often been blamed himself. He says of Wordsworth's descriptions of scenery that they were "interspersed with dialogues which, though they proceeded from the mouths of pedlars and rustics, were of the most edifying description; mostly on subjects moral or metaphysical, and couched in the most gentlemanly and unexceptionable language, without the slightest mixture of vulgarity, coarseness or pie-bald grammar" (*The Romany Rye*, I, 218).

43. Compare the dialogue recorded in *Lavengro*, I, 51-52, where Borrow, though a child of six or eight, is represented as speaking in the language and with the sentiments of a grown man.

44. Letter of June 7, 1842. Quoted Knapp, I, 387.

45. (Feb. 1843), p. 76.

46. *Res Judicatae* (1892), p. 118.

47. *Through the Magic Door* (1908), p. 63.

48. *Obiter Dicta* (1902), p. 260. See *The Bible*, I, 179 for a typical example.

49. *Essays in English Literature* (1891), p. 434.

50. Martin Armstrong, *George Borrow* (1950), p. 57.

51. *Dublin University Magazine* (Feb., 1843), p. 248; *Quarterly Review* (March, 1843), p. 197; *Post Liminium: Essays and Critical Papers* (1912), p. 202.

52. *Op. cit.*, p. 409.

53. *Danger! And Other Stories* (1911), p. 167.

54. Quoted Knapp, II, 11. (Letter dated Nov. 6, 1843).

55. *Op. cit.*, pp. 414-15.

56. "Recollections of George Borrow," *Athenaeum* (Aug. 13, 1881), pp. 203-4.

57. March, 1843, p. 362.

58. *The Bible*, I, 418; *Lavengro*, I, 202. Good examples occur also in *The Bible*, I, 199-200; II, 305-6.

59. *Athenaeum* (Sept. 3, 1881), p. 301.

60. *Dublin Review* (March, 1914), p. 59.

61. *Through the Magic Door* (1908), pp. 97-98.

62. June, 1851, p. 144.

63. The student of Borrow reads and re-reads this extract as he plows through critical reviews and general articles until he begins to need Peter Quennell to tell him that "in its proper context Jasper Petulengro's references to the wind upon the heath loses its air of having been specially composed for a Christmas gift-calendar or cheap-jack prose anthology" (*The Singular Preference*, 1952, p. 145). Edd Winfield Parks, *Segments of Southern Thought* (1938), p. 316, recalls having been introduced to it by Charles Townsend Copeland at Harvard and thought of it as "one of the finest passages in literature." For still other examples of Borrow's Romantic style, see *The Bible*, II, 53, 322; *Lavengro*, I, 10, 15, 70, 119, 138-39; II, 163, 207-13.

Chapter Four

1. *Eclectic Review* (May, 1851), p. 446.

2. Robert Morss Lovett and Helen Sard Hughes, *The History of the Novel in England* (1932), p. 286.

3. *A History of English Prose Rhythm* (1912), p. 143.

4. Amy Cruse, *The Englishman and His Books in the Early 19th Century* (n.d.), p. 15.

5. Augustus Ralli, *Critiques* (1927), p. 133.

6. *The Literary Impact of the Authorized Version* (1950), p. 16.

7. *The Bible in Spain*, II, 76, 130; *Lavengro*, I, 162; II, 7 for widely scattered examples.

8. *Loc. cit.*

9. *Athenaeum* (Aug. 13, 1881), p. 209. Herbert Jenkins, *The Life of George Borrow* (1924), also testifies to Borrow's knowledge of Hebrew, at pp. 31, 34, and 142.

10. *Ibid.*

Chapter Five

1. Martin Armstrong, *George Borrow* (1950), p. 96.
2. *English Review*, XV (1843), p. 377.
3. Arthur Rickett, *The Vagabond in Literature* (1906), p. 84.
4. *Encyclopaedia Britannica*, Eleventh Edition, IV, 275.
5. *Athenaeum* (Sept. 10, 1881), p. 337.
6. Edward Thomas, *George Borrow* (1912), p. 206.
7. To Dawson Turner, dated Jan. 15. Included in Knapp, I, 393-94.
8. *Harper's* (Nov., 1914), p. 958.
9. John Macy, *The Critical Game* (1922), p. 254.
10. This habit is discussed by Edward Thomas, *op. cit.*, pp. 250 ff.
11. *Times Literary Supplement* (April 22, 1939), p. 229. The biography is Seton Dearden's *The Gypsy Gentleman* (1939).
12. *Harper's* (Nov., 1914), p. 959.
13. Letter to Don Luis de Usoz y Rio, a Spanish friend. Quoted by Armstrong, *op. cit.*, p. 90.
14. Letter to Don Luis. Translated in Knapp, II, 287.

Chapter Six

1. *The Broad Highway*, p. 1.
2. *Ibid.*, p. 2.
3. *The Nation*, Aug. 8, 1912, pp. 122-23.
4. *A History of the English Novel*. Vol. IX, 334.
5. Wilbur Cross, *The Development of the English Novel* (New York, 1937), p. 283.
6. Keith Hollingsworth, *The Newgate Novel, 1830-1847* (Detroit, 1963). Hollingsworth traces the Newgate theme through Bulwer, Ainsworth, Dickens, and Thackeray, but he gives Borrow only the briefest mention.
7. *A History of the English Novel*. Vol. VIII, 177.
8. Konrad Bercovici, "George Borrow's Gypsies," *New York Evening Post* (Aug. 27, 1921), p. 2.
9. *Letters of Sherwood Anderson*. Ed. Howard Mumford Jones (Boston, 1953), p. 431.

Chapter Seven

1. *Athenaeum* (Aug. 6, 1881), p. 177.
2. C. M. Bowen, "George Borrow," *Westminster Review* (March, 1910), p. 304.

3. John E. Tilford, "The Critical Approach to *Lavengro-Romany Rye*," *Studies in Philology*, XLVI (Jan., 1949), 79-96; and "The Formal Artistry of *Lavengro-Romany Rye*," *Publication of the Modern Language Association*, LXIV (June, 1949), 369-84.

4. *Danger! And Other Stories* (New York, 1911), pp. 163-66.

Selected Bibliography

The following bibliography lists Borrow's important primary works, and lists also some of the useful biographical, critical, and miscellaneous materials which a student would want to consult. Lists of the various editions and reprints of Borrow's works are not included; these are easily available in the following places: T. J. Wise, *A Bibliography of the Writings in Prose and Verse of George Henry Borrow* (London, 1914); George F. Black, *Gypsy Bibliography* (Edinburgh, 1914); G. A. Stephen, *Borrow House Museum: A Brief Account of the Life of George Borrow and His Norwich Home, With a Bibliography* (Norwich, 1927); and William I. Knapp's *Life,* listed below.

PRIMARY SOURCES

The Works of George Borrow. Edited, With Much Hitherto Unpublished Manuscript, by Clement Shorter. Norwich Edition, 16 Vols. London: Constable, 1923-24.
I-II: *The Bible in Spain.*
III-IV: *Lavengro.*
V-VI: *The Romany Rye.*
VII-IX: *The Songs of Scandinavia, and Other Poems and Ballads.*
X: *The Zincali.*
XI: *Romano Lavo-Lil.*
XII-XIV: *Wild Wales.*
XV-XVI: *Miscellanies.*

Celebrated Trials and Remarkable Cases of Criminal Jurisprudence from the Earliest Records to the Year 1825. Ed. George Borrow. 5 Vols. London: privately printed for the Navarre Society, Ltd., 1925-26.

Letters of George Borrow to the British and Foreign Bible Society. Ed. T. H. Darlow. London: Hodder and Stoughton, 1911.

SECONDARY SOURCES

1. Biographies and Critical Studies

ADAMS, MORLEY. *In The Footsteps of Borrow and Fitzgerald.* London: Jarrold and Sons, 1915. A casual ramble through the East Anglian countryside done in the anecdotal style of the travelogue. Among many photographs is a reproduction of the only known one of Borrow.

ARMSTRONG, MARTIN. *George Borrow.* London: William Claves and Sons, 1950. Views Borrow's books as psychological documents. Finds Borrow egotistical and a victim of crippling mental instabilities. Says Borrow's sexual inadequacy produced his warped personality.

CRENSHAW, TROY CLAY. "George Borrow and the Borrovian Cult." Unpublished dissertation (University of Texas, 1937). Traces origin, influence, and death of the circle of dedicated admirers. Pays some attention to Borrow's artistry.

DEARDEN, SETON. *The Gypsy Gentleman.* London: John Murray, 1939. Popular, eulogistic.

ELAM, SAMUEL MILTON. *George Borrow.* New York: Alfred A. Knopf, 1929. Charming personal reaction to Borrow. Most memorable assertion: that the interlude with Isopel Berners in the dell was *not* Platonic and that it is unfair to Borrow to take him at his word on this matter.

HOPKINS, R. THURSTON. *George Borrow: Lord of the Open Road.* London: Jarrold and Sons, 1922. The title is not misleading: Borrow's magnificent physical endowments and religious devotion to hiking are exploited fully.

JENKINS, HERBERT. *The Life of George Borrow.* London: John Murray, 1924. Accurate, detailed, and readable. One of the best of the biographies. Adds a few new (and mostly unimportant) letters to Knapp's classic. One minor accomplishment: Jenkins straightens out the conflicting accounts of Borrow's association with Lieutenant Graydon.

KNAPP, WILLIAM I. *Life, Writings and Correspondence of George Borrow, Based on Official and Other Authentic Sources.* 2 Vols. London: John Murray, 1899. Comprehensive, indispensable, highly dependable encyclopedia of every fact Dr. Knapp could uncover. Borrow research begins with this work.

NORTHAM, STUART. "An Analysis of the Methods of Fiction Used by George Borrow." Unpublished dissertation (Denver University, 1954). Tries to determine the extent of Borrow's creative imagination. Studies the letters sent back from Spain to the Bible Society and indicates *The Bible in Spain*'s dependence on them.

SHORTER, CLEMENT. *George Borrow and His Circle.* London: Hodder and Stoughton, 1913. Shorter's access to private letters and personal papers, and his use of other previously unprinted documents, make this study valuable. An ardent Borrovian, Shorter fills his book with letters.

————. *The Life of George Borrow.* New York: E. P. Dutton, 1928. A re-issue of the above, in expanded form.

THOMAS, EDWARD. *George Borrow: The Man and His Books.* London: Chapman and Hall, 1912. By Mr. Thomas' own admission "only a re-arrangement" of materials. Copious illustrations. No critical analysis.

TILFORD, JOHN E. "George Borrow as a Literary Artist." Unpublished dissertation (University of Michigan, 1942). The best purely critical examination of Borrow's works.

VESEY-FITZGERALD, BRIAN. *Gypsy Borrow.* London: Dobson, 1953. Explains Borrow's powers and perversities on the basis that he was a full-blooded gypsy. Eccentricities not thus accounted for are taken care of by stressing Borrow's Cornish ancestry.

WALLING, R. A. J. *George Borrow: The Man and His Work.* London: Cassell and Co., 1908. Explains Borrow's life and works on the basis of his Celtic origin. New material: some correspondence which throws light on the "Veiled Period."

2. Essays and Books Containing References to Borrow

ANDERSON, SHERWOOD. *Hello, Towns!* New York: H. Liveright, 1929.

BIRRELL, AUGUSTINE. *Res Judicatae: Papers and Essays.* New York: Scribner, 1892.

————. *More Obiter Dicta.* New York: Scribner, 1924.

BRACE, CHARLES L. *Hungary in 1851.* New York: Scribner, 1853.

DOUGLAS, JAMES. *Theodore Watts-Dunton.* London: Lane, 1904.

DOYLE, ARTHUR C. *Danger! And Other Stories.* New York: Burt, 1911.

————. *Through the Magic Door.* New York: Doubleday, 1908.

FINDLATER, JANE H. *Stones From a Glass House.* London: James Nisbet and Co., 1904.

GILBERT, ALLAN H. *Literary Criticism: Plato to Dryden.* New York: American Book Co., 1940.

HAKE, GORDON. *Memoirs of 80 Years.* London: R. Bentley and Son, 1892.

HAKE, THOMAS AND COMPTON-RICKETT, ARTHUR. *Life and Letters of Theodore Watts-Dunton.* 2 Vols. New York: G. P. Putnam's Sons, 1916.

HEARN, LAFCADIO. *Some Strange English Figures of the Early 19th Century.* Tokyo: Hokuseido, n.d.

HENLEY, W. E. *Views and Reviews: Essays in Appreciation.* London: Scribner, 1890.

JOHNSON, LIONEL. *Post Liminium: Essays and Critical Papers*, ed. Thomas Whittemore. London: E. Matthews, 1911.

JONES, HOWARD MUMFORD, ed. *Letters of Sherwood Anderson*. Boston: Little, Brown and Co., 1953.

MACY, JOHN. *The Critical Game*. New York: Boni and Liveright, 1922.

MARTINEAU, HARRIETT. *Autobiography*, ed. Maria W. Chapman. 2 Vols. Boston: J. R. Osgood and Co., 1877.

MILFORD, HUMPHREY S., ed. *Borrow Selections*. Oxford: Oxford University Press, 1928.

MILLER, BETTY, ed. *Elizabeth Barrett to Miss Mitford*. London: John Murray, 1954.

MORE, PAUL ELMER. *The Demon of the Absolute*. Princeton: Princeton University Press, 1928.

PARKS, EDD WINFIELD. "Portrait of Lavengro: A Biographical Essay on George Borrow." *Segments of Southern Thought*. Athens: University of Georgia Press, 1938.

PROTHERO, ROWLAND E., ed. *The Letters of Richard Ford*. New York: E. P. Dutton, 1905.

QUENNELL, PETER. *The Singular Preference: Portraits and Essays*. London: Collins, 1952.

RALLI, AUGUSTUS. *Critiques*. London: Longmans, Greene and Co., 1927.

RICKETT, ARTHUR. *Personal Forces in Modern Literature*. London: J. M. Dent, 1906.

———. *The Vagabond in Literature*. London: J. M. Dent, 1906.

SAINTSBURY, GEORGE. *Essays in English Literature, 1780-1860*. London: Rivington, Percival and Co., 1896.

SECCOMBE, THOMAS. Introduction to *The Bible in Spain*. Everyman Edition. London: J. M. Dent, 1891.

SMILES, SAMUEL. *Brief Biographies*. Boston: Ticknor and Fields, 1861.

South Atlantic Studies for Sturgis E. Leavitt, ed. Thomas B. Stroup and Sterling A. Stoudemire. Washington: Scarecrow, 1953.

THOMAS, EDWARD. Intro. to *The Bible in Spain* (Everyman's). London: J. M. Dent, 1907.

WATTS-DUNTON, THEODORE. Intro. to *Wild Wales* (Everyman's). London: J. M. Dent, 1907.

3. Periodicals

"Another Life of Borrow," *The Nation* (Nov., 1914), 333-34.

"Borrow and His Times," *Bookman* (May, 1913), 15-18.

"The Borrow Revival," *The Outlook* (Jan. 5, 1901), 55-58.

BOWEN, C. M. "George Borrow," *Westminster Review* (March, 1910), 286-304.

Selected Bibliography

BOYLE, ANDREW. "Portraiture in 'Lavengro,'" *Cornhill Magazine* (March, 1928), 317-24.

BOYNTON, H. W. "George Borrow," *The Atlantic Monthly* (Feb., 1904), 244-53.

ELWIN, WHITWELL. "Mr. Borrow," *Athenaeum* (Aug. 6, 1881), 177.

"George Borrow," *Living Age* (Dec. 20, 1913), 712-23.

"George Borrow," *London Times Literary Supplement* (Aug. 28, 1924), 517-18.

HAKE, A. EGMONT. "George Borrow," *Living Age* (Oct., 1881), 558-560.

————. "Recollections of George Borrow," *Athenaeum* (Aug. 13, 1881), 201-10.

HOWELLS, WILLIAM DEAN. "In the Editor's Easy Chair," *Harper's* (Nov., 1914), 958-61.

HUNT, SIR JOHN. "Triumph on Everest," *The National Geographic Magazine* (July, 1954), 35.

JESSOP, AUGUSTUS. "Lavengro," *Athenaeum* (July 8, 1893), 65-66.

McGUIRE, OWEN B. "Spain, A Century Ago," *The Commonweal* (July 5, 1940), 220-22.

MORE, PAUL ELMER. "George Borrow," *The Nation* (June 27, 1912), 633-36.

RALLI, AUGUSTUS. "George Borrow," *Fortnightly Review* (Oct. 1, 1915), 711-24.

SCHEVILLE, RUDOLPH. "George Borrow, English Humorist in Spain," *University of California Chronicle* (May, 1916), 1-24.

SHANE, LESLIE. "George Borrow in Spain," *Dublin Review* (March, 1914), 42-59.

TILFORD, JOHN E. "The Critical Approach to *Lavengro-Romany Rye*," *Studies in Philology*, XLVI (Jan., 1949), 79-96.

————. "The Formal Artistry of *Lavengro-Romany Rye*," *Publ. of the Modern Language Association*, LXIV (June, 1949), 369-84.

TRILLING, LIONEL. "A Ramble on Graves," *The Griffin* (June, 1955), 6.

WATTS-DUNTON, THEODORE. "Reminiscences of George Borrow," *Athenaeum* (Sept. 3, 1881), 307-8; and (Sept. 10, 1881), 336-38.

Index

Hudson, William Henry, 130
Hunt, Sir John, 7

Jenkins, Herbert, 65
Jessop, Augustus, 26

Kieran, John, 7
Knapp, William I., 65, 137

Leslie, Shane, 102
LeSage, Alain Rene, 46, 47, 121
Lewis, C. S., 109, 110
Lockhart, John Gibson, 62

Macy, John, 71
Martineau, Harriet, 140
McGuire, Owen, 67, 78
Meredith, George, 10, 130
More, Paul Elmer, 77
Murray, John, 7, 20, 24, 25, 26, 33, 98, 116, 119

Old Crome, 81
Oulton, 14, 19, 20, 32, 39
Oxford Movement, 58

Parks, Edd Winfield, 146
Peel, Sir Robert, 26
Phillips, Sir Richard, 13, 18, 28, 143
Picaresque, 6, 44-47, 123, 124, 130
Putnam, Nina Wilcox, 128

Quennell, Peter, 146
Quesada, 23

Ralli, Augustus, 75
Richmond, Leigh, 59
Robberds, F. W., 107

Saintsbury, George, 43, 70, 86, 88, 89, 97, 98-99, 108
Salmon, David, 65
Scott, Walter, 10, 13, 23, 35, 36, 37, 125, 134
Shorter, Clement, 65
Shorthouse, J. H., 74
Smiles, Samuel, 26
Smollett, Tobias George, 10, 25, 120, 123-24
Stephen, G. A., 6
Stevenson, Lionel, 6
Stevenson, Robert Louis, 10, 130
Sterne, Laurence, 10, 76, 120, 124

Taylor, William, 13, 28, 57, 90, 100
Trilling, Lionel, 8

"Veiled Period" (Borrow's), 14, 18, 151
Vesey-Fitzgerald, Brian, 7
Villiers, 52, 53

Watts-Dunton, Theodore, 10, 39, 55, 62, 73, 85, 91, 92, 101, 118, 127, 129
Waugh, Arthur, 137
Wellek, Rene, 75
Woodbridge, Homer, 128-29
Wordsworth, William, 10, 35